# In Praise of Reason

# In Praise of Reason

Michael P. Lynch

The MIT Press
Cambridge, Massachusetts
London, England

MIT Press books may be purchased at special quantity discounts for business or sales promotional use. For information, please email special _sales@mitpress.mit.edu or write to Special Sales Department, The MIT Press, 55 Hayward Street, Cambridge, MA 02142.

This book was set in Stone Sans and Stone Serif by Toppan Best-set Premedia Limited. Printed and bound in the United States of America.

Library of Congress Cataloging-in-Publication Data

Lynch, Michael P. (Michael Patrick), 1966–.
In praise of reason / Michael P. Lynch.
   p.  cm.
Includes bibliographical references (p.   ) and index.
ISBN 978-0-262-01722-0 (hardcover : alk. paper)
1. Reason. 2. Reasoning. 3. Rationalism. I. Title.
B833.L96   2012
128'.33—dc23
2011038298

10   9   8   7   6   5   4   3   2   1

For Patty

# Contents

# Preface

Imagine that a mysteriously powerful scientist offers you a choice between two doors. Behind door number one is the ability to slowly convince many of your political opponents of the wisdom of your views by appeal to reason. Behind door number two is a serum that, once slipped into the water supply, will quickly make "the other side" think your political views are the right ones. Which door would you choose?

Most folks I know, including myself, would be at least tempted to choose the magic serum. And many people would choose it immediately, without much thought. After all, politics concerns matters of serious import, and it is hard *not* to wish that those on the other side would either go away or be magically transformed into what we consider to be right-thinking people. It is easy to think that would be for the greater good. But even so, you might hesitate. There is something clearly wrong about manipulating people into unconsciously agreeing with you, even when the stakes are high and it would get the job done quickly and efficiently. We think there is something valuable in appealing to reasons. The process of giving and asking for reasons *matters*, independently of what it may happen to get us.

Of course, the value of appealing to reasons also depends on whether they are *good* reasons. Good reasons are based on good principles. So the aim of this book is to defend both the value of giving reasons in public discourse and the value of certain principles over others—in particular, the principles that constitute a scientific approach to the world. Appealing to these principles in public discourse matters, I argue, despite the fact that there appear to be—perversely enough—very good reasons to think that we can't defend them with noncircular reasons. It sometimes seems as if every "first principle" ends up being founded on something else that is arbitrary: emotion, faith, or plain prejudice. If that's so, then a magic serum is the best we could hope for after all. Nonetheless, I'll try to convince you that we can hope for more.

This problem of the value of reason is one of the oldest philosophical problems. And like many deep philosophical problems, it is not purely academic. Solutions to it have wider consequences for our culture. This book is an attempt, and no doubt an imperfect and incomplete attempt, to grapple with this problem. But it is also an invitation to take the problem seriously, and to join in trying to solve it.

In the philosophical literature, "skepticism" is mostly associated with the idea that we lack knowledge. My own interest in the value of reason arises partly from a longstanding suspicion that the real interest in skepticism lies not in its consequences (or lack thereof) for our understanding of knowledge, but in the challenge it poses to the importance of reasoning and the practice of exchanging reasons. In my view, knowledge is often less important than philosophers tend to think. What matters most is being able to defend and articulate that knowledge.

My thinking on these subjects has many influences. These include certain themes of American pragmatism, and the naturalist yet humanist stance I find in John Dewey, C. S. Peirce, and William James. Another is the work of the late William Alston, my mentor and friend, whose pioneering work on epistemic circularity introduced me to these problems. I am still arguing with Bill, even now. Other writers who have had a significant impact on my thought include Ernest Sosa, Crispin Wright, and Michael Williams. Over the last six years, many other people have helped me with the ideas in this book, either in conversation or by comments on the manuscript. They include Donald Baxter, Robert Barnard, Paul Bloomfield, Tom Bontly, David Capps, Nancy Daukas, Michael Fuerstein, Patrick Greenough, Eberhard Herrmann, Klemens Kappel, Hilary Kornblith, Scott Lehmann, Bridget Lynch, Patty Lynch, Christopher McEnroe, N. J. L. L. Pedersen, Tom Polger, Duncan Pritchard, Paul Silva, Kent Stephens, John Troyer, Steven Wall, and Jeremy Wyatt. I also profited from presenting lectures based on this material at numerous places, including the University of Alabama, the University of Cincinnati, Fordham University, University College Dublin, Edinburgh University, Tufts University, University of St. Andrews, the University of Copenhagen, the American Philosophical Association, and the University of Aberdeen. Portions of chapter 4 derive from "Epistemic Circularity and Epistemic Incommensurability," in *Social Epistemology*, ed. A. Haddock, A. Millar, and D. Pritchard (Oxford: Oxford University Press, 2010); while parts of chapter 5 were originally published under the title "Truth and the Pathos of Distance" in *The Philosophy of Richard Rorty*, ed. R. Auxier (Chicago: Open Court, 2010).

Special thanks go to my agent, Peter Matson, and to two of MIT Press's editors, Tom Stone, who began the project, and

Philip Laughlin, who saw it through. Thanks to all three for believing, and apologies for taking so long.

Finally, I end with special thanks to Terry, who remains, as always, my beacon of reason and love.

Storrs, Connecticut
August 2011

# 1 Hope and Reason

## 1 Sources of Skepticism

One of the best-selling books of the last decade advises its readers that "AIDS is one of the greatest hoaxes" ever pulled on Americans.[1] Some people continue to think that the MMR vaccine causes autism. Others, including some leading American politicians and news commentators, believe that global warming is a myth. And many more than that—perhaps most Americans, in fact—believe that creationism should be taught in secondary school science classrooms alongside the theory of natural selection.

Some who believe these things may do so because they sincerely believe that the scientific evidence supports their position. But for most people, scientific evidence has little to do with it. Take the case of evolution. According to a 2007 Gallup poll, only 14 percent of those who said they did not believe in evolution cited lack of evidence as the main reason for their view.[2] Other polls indicate that most people are aware that there is overwhelming scientific agreement on the truth of evolutionary theory. In other words, it is not that people think that there isn't *scientific* evidence for evolutionary theory,[3] it is that this sort of evidence isn't persuasive to them when it comes to many of the issues they really care about. When asked what they would do if scientists were to "disprove" a particular religious belief, nearly two-thirds of the people asked said they would continue to hold that religious belief anyway.[4]

Commentators have drawn a number of lessons from these facts, ranging from the sociological (people don't feel invested in science) to the psychological (certain ideas are easier to digest than others). These explanations have their merits, but they overlook another possibility: that many people are just highly skeptical about *reason*. The causes of this skepticism are varied, but underlying all of them is a common thought: that all "rational" explanations end up grounding out on something arbitrary. In the end, it all just comes down to what you happen to believe, what you feel in your gut, or blind faith. This is a powerful idea—in part because it contains more than a grain of truth, and in part because it simply feels liberating. It levels the playing field, intellectually speaking. After all, if all reasons are grounded on something arbitrary, then why assume science is on any firmer foundation than anything else? You might as well just go with what you believe even if it contradicts the evidence.

Yet like many powerful ideas, this one turns poisonous when taken to its logical limit. The thought that everything is arbitrary undermines a key principle of a civil society: that we owe our fellow citizens explanations for what we do. Civil societies are not necessarily polite or homogeneous; but they are societies that value reason-giving, inquiry, questioning, and hashing out one's differences with others. In so doing, they take seriously the idea that there are better and worse ways of doing these things. If you give up on the idea that there are standards of this sort, you give up on the idea that giving reasons has any real point. Deliberation becomes a game played for the joy of manipulation and the increase of power. Skepticism about reason undermines our commitment to civil society, and that is why it is important to understand its causes and answer its arguments.

That is what I aim to do in this book. I will try to convince you that while skeptical worries are serious and in many ways understandable, they can be answered. Reason matters and *appeals* to reasons matter, and not just for the noble ideals of the academy, but for the down-to-brass-tacks, mud-on-your-boots world in which we all live.

What do I mean by "reason"? In the broadest sense of the term, reason is the ability to explain and justify our beliefs and commitments. So, to provide *a* reason for something is to justify or explain it. But "reason" is often employed in a slightly narrower way as well. In this narrower sense, "using reason" means using certain methods, appealing to certain sources, and engaging in certain practices over others. This includes, most obviously, logical inference (both "deductive" and "inductive") and what is often called "observation"—inference from perceptual experience.[5] It is in this sense that we take scientific practice to be an exemplar of reason: it is committed to certain principles that privilege the methods of observation and logic.[6]

Skeptical worries about reason concern this narrower sense. They have three main sources. The first is just the suspicion that all reasoning is ultimately "rationalization"—retrospective work that's done after our emotions have already committed us. Ironically, support for this skeptical thought has recently come from science itself. Some researchers have argued that a growing amount of data from the psychological sciences indicates that reason doesn't play much of a causal role in our lives. What does play such a role is our sentiments and feelings; and consequently, it is those things that really matter, not reason itself. Reason is not causally efficacious.

A second, and subtler, source of skepticism is that we can't give reasons for our trust in reason without running in circles. How do we defend our trust in science, goes the challenge—with more science? That seems to some like defending the trustworthiness of a car salesman by having him swear that he always tells the truth. On the cultural Right in America, the fact that reason is circular in this way is sometimes taken to prove that science is "just another faith." It is on equal, or perhaps even lower, standing with religion. Strikingly, there are some on the cultural Left who conclude from the same premises that scientific methods are just one type of methodology among others, and that there is no principled way to choose between them. Reasons are, to use a tired word, "relative," dictated by our culture or dependent on the vagaries of our individual psychologies.

This second source of skepticism has its origins in ancient Greek philosophy. That itself signals a deep ambivalence toward reason in Western civilization. Greece is the birthplace of philosophy and the dream of reason; but it is also the place where the followers of Pyrrho, four centuries before Christ, first argued that reason can't defend itself. And skepticism about reason later became part of early Christian thought, prompting Tertullian's notorious query, "What has Athens to do with Jerusalem?"— which means something like: What has reason to do with faith? So while the West has long claimed bragging rights for having institutionalized the role of reason in society, it has also fostered skepticism about that role.

The third source of skepticism about reason is that it operates under a false pretense: it claims to reveal the objective truth. But to many people across the cultural spectrum, objective truth is an illusion—useful and productive, perhaps, but an illusion all the same. Best to give up believing in truth and so accept that neither reason *nor* anything else can reveal it to us. This is a view familiar to anyone who, like myself, went to college and graduate school in the 1980s and 1990s. In those heady days, the rejection of the "meta-narrative" of Enlightenment rationalism was seen—not without irony—as the one true triumph of postmodernism.

Postmodernism is no longer the "it-girl" of the academy, and by and large I think this is a good thing. Yet the criticisms that many of its advocates raised against Enlightenment rationalism were real and important. I will not defend reason with a capital R, nor the illusion that reason is value-free—nor that there are unfounded foundations, nor that there is a bare, unbiased "given" in experience. My defense of reason is naturalist. It takes its inspiration as much from some of reason's critics, such as David Hume, as it does from its more ardent supporters, such as Plato. Like the American pragmatists, I think the best we can say on behalf of reason—indeed, what we should say—is that it plays a central role in any healthy public culture.

This book is also not intended as an attack on religion or spirituality. The question here is not whether God exists. Nor am I interested in debunking "faith"—at least in the sense of that troubled word that means "believing without explicit evidence." Indeed, I think that we sometimes have no choice but to accept some principles without evidence. That's not the problem. The problem is thinking that this means that we can't give reasons for those principles, and hence that we should be ambivalent about reason in public discourse. That is a really bad idea, and it is not hard to see why.

## 2  Democracy as a Space of Reasons

The state of Texas buys or distributes 48 million textbooks annually in its public schools. As such, it largely dictates what is to be found in most public school textbooks across the United States. So it is not surprising that there is a lot of attention paid to what goes into those books; indeed, their contents are at the center of some of the deepest cultural debates in the country. One of these is the debate over whether creationism should be taught to children as a legitimate scientific theory about the origin of life. Some members of the Texas State Board of Education have expressed the view that it should be taught, arguing that, among other things, there is a scientific conspiracy to hide both flaws in the theory of evolution and evidence for the idea that the earth and all its inhabitants were created by a Christian God. Another debate is over the founding and history of the United States. Various members of the Board of Education and their advocates continue to lobby, often successfully, for including language in history textbooks that emphasizes what they believe to be true: that the United States was founded with the intention of being a "Christian Nation" and, moreover, that its founding was providentially guided by God.[7]

The case of the Texas State Board of Education provides an interesting example of how skepticism about reason can work its way into very practical matters. This is not to say that highfalutin' debates about skepticism were on the table during the Board's *actual* decisions about what to include and what not to include in their textbooks. Those decisions are doubtless the result of a variety of causes—mostly political, and many local. But whatever the disputants' real motivation for their views, the disagreement isn't only about politics. It isn't even just about the facts. It is also about how best to go about learning about the facts—about what we might call our epistemic principles. *Moral principles* tell us what is rational to do. *Epistemic principles* tell us what is rational to believe, including which methods of belief we should trust and value the most. This question, the question of which epistemic principles we should have, is what gives local debates like those in Texas a larger meaning in our national culture. And it raises a fundamental worry: How do we resolve disagreements over values like this? What sort of reasons can we appeal to in order to make our case?

Some people I know shrug off such questions. Why, they ask, should *I* care about convincing people who don't share my epistemic principles, who don't understand the obvious fact that science is always the better method for knowing about matters like the origin of life on this planet? Again, epistemic principles tell us what is rational to believe. So anyone who doubts *my basic epistemic principles* is going to appear to *me* as someone who doubts the rules of rationality. So, why should I care about what they think? It's not as if they'll be able to recognize my (good) reasons anyway, and to me, *their* "reasons" will not be legitimate.[8]

But what counts as "legitimate"? There's the rub. A legitimate challenge is presumably a rational challenge. Disagreements over epistemic principles are disagreements over which methods and sources to trust, in short, over what is rational to believe. And there we have the problem. We can't decide on what counts as a legitimate reason to doubt my methods unless we've already settled on which methods to trust—and that is the very issue in question. The problem that skepticism about reason raises is not about whether I have good evidence by my principles for my principles. Presumably I do. The problem is whether I can give a more objective defense of them. That is, whether I can give reasons for them that can be appreciated from what Hume called a "common point of view"—reasons that can "move some universal principle of the human frame, and touch a string, to which all mankind have an accord and symphony."[9]

I think that we ignore this problem—the problem of defending our epistemic principles from a common point of view—at our peril. It is not that I think we should come up with a list of bullet-points to convince people to employ scientific reason in public discourse. That would be a waste of time. Nor is my point that it is *politically* stupid to dismiss other people's viewpoints in a democratic society. (Although it is. You don't help your message by displaying a haughty indifference to others' challenges.) My point is that defending some of our epistemic principles, our faith in reason, is required by some of our other principles. Hume's point, in alluding to what he also sometimes called "the principle of humanity," was that the ideal of civility requires us to find common ground with those with whom we must discuss practical matters. More recent political philosophers like John Rawls and Jürgen Habermas have seen this ideal as a key component of a functioning liberal democracy. In this view, democracies aren't simply organizing a struggle for power between competing interests; democratic politics isn't war by other means. Democracies are, or should be, spaces of reasons. In the words of the political philosopher Joshua Cohen, a democracy is an association whose justification "proceeds through public argument and reasoning among equal citizens."[10] Democracies are essentially set up to allow for mutual deliberation involving the exchange of public reasons—reasons that can be recognized by standards other than your own.[11] As the political philosopher Jean Hampton once put it: "No matter what our religion, moral beliefs, or metaphysical commitments, if we are to work together in one system of cooperation, we have to have a 'common currency' for debating and settling disputes or our society will be in ruins."[12]

So one reason we should take the project of defending our epistemic principles seriously is that the ideal of civility demands it. But there is also another, even deeper, reason. We need to justify our epistemic principles from a common point of view because we need shared epistemic principles in order to even have a common point of view. Without a common background of standards against which we measure what counts as a reliable source of information, or a reliable method of inquiry, and what doesn't, we won't be able *to agree on the facts*, let alone values. Indeed, this is precisely the situation we seem to be headed toward in the United States. We live isolated in our separate bubbles of information culled from sources that only reinforce our prejudices and never challenge our basic assumptions. No wonder that we so often fail to reach agreement, as the Texas school board case illustrates, over the history and physical structure of the world itself. No wonder joint action grinds to a halt. When you can't agree on your principles of evidence and rationality, you can't agree on the facts. And if you can't agree on the facts, you can hardly agree on what to do in the face of the facts.

Put simply, we need an epistemic common currency because we often have to decide, jointly, what to do in the face of disagreement.[13] Sometimes we can accomplish this, in a democratic society, by voting. But we can't decide every issue that way, and we certainly can't decide on our epistemic principles—which methods and sources are *actually* rationally worthy of trust—by voting. We need some forms of common currency before we get to the voting booth. And that means that we need to face up to skepticism about reason. Skepticism about reason isn't just a matter of questioning whether we actually have shared standards of rationality. After all, we already know that we don't. What skepticism threatens is the very *possibility* of ever sharing epistemic principles. As such, it raises the worry that we can't hope to share a common point of view in general, and in so doing, threatens a central tenet of a civil, democratic way of life.

In his most famous conservative manifesto, philosopher Michael Oakeshott described his liberal opponent (whom he called "The Rationalist") in this way:

His circumstances in the modern world have made him contentious: he is the enemy of authority, of prejudice, of the merely traditional, customary or habitual. His mental attitude is at once skeptical and optimistic . . . Moreover, he is fortified by a belief in a "reason" common to all mankind, a common power of rational consideration, which is the ground and inspiration of argument; set up on his door is the precept of Parmenides—judge by rational argument.[14]

Oakeshott, apparently, takes this to be a damning indictment; and if so, then I plead guilty as charged. I confess I still have hope in reason. But the hope I have in reason is in human reason—a reason that is marked with frailty, fed by our sentiments and passions, whose pale promethean flame must be cultivated lest it gutter and dim. This book is an attempt to show that this hope is justified.

# 2 Neither Slave nor Master: Reason and Emotion

## 1 Alarming Data

In the fall of 2007, researchers from Princeton announced some apparently disturbing results: a split-second glance at two candidates' faces is often enough to predict who will win an election.[1] In previous work, Alexander Todorov and his colleagues had provided convincing evidence that people judge the competence of an unfamiliar face within a tenth of a second. That alone is something: it shows that people make such judgments prior to consciously reflecting on them. But in the later study, Todorov and Charles Ballew decided to look into how such judgments might correlate with election results.

In one experiment, the scientists presented college students with the faces of the Democratic and Republican candidates for each of the 2006 gubernatorial and Senate races—two weeks *prior* to the election. The students were asked for their "gut feeling" about which person was more competent. Only responses from participants who did not recognize either face were included in the analysis, thus ensuring that their snap judgment was based only on appearance. After the election, these scientists correlated their findings with the election results and found that participants' judgments had predicted the winners in *72.4 percent of the senatorial races and 68.6 percent of the gubernatorial races—even when the students were given less than 100 ms to see the candidates' faces.* Moreover, asking the participants to deliberate about their judgments not only didn't increase their ability to predict election results, it generally lowered it, causing the authors to note that "what predicts the outcomes of elections is the automatic component of trait judgments. Deliberation instructions add noise to automatic trait judgments and, consequently, reduce the accuracy of prediction."[2] In other words, many people may make their political judgments unreflectively, even on appearance alone. Thinking only gets in the way.

These results are actually just a small part of a growing scientific industry studying how we make both moral and political decisions.[3] And the lesson that many observers are drawing from it is worth thinking about. I don't mean the fact that most folks' political and ethical decisions are emotionally loaded, based on meager information, and often less than reasoned out. *That* would hardly be surprising, as anyone from Machiavelli to Karl Rove could tell you. The more interesting conclusion is that reason has almost nothing to do with our decisions, political or otherwise. When it comes to figuring out what we want to do, or even what we believe is true, *reason is simply beside the point.*

A particularly vigorous advocate of this way of seeing the recent data is the neuroscientist turned political consultant Drew Westen. Westen, author of the bestselling *The Political Brain*, has himself reported some interesting results. In one study, Westen and his colleagues studied the brain activity of liberal and conservative political partisans during the 2004 presidential election.[4] Each participant was confronted with the same number of contradictory statements from John Kerry and George W. Bush. After being given time to think about it, participants were then asked to say which of the statements were really contradictory. Westen and his colleagues scanned the participants' brains (using fMRI techniques) during the entire process. Unsurprisingly, the political partisans tended overwhelmingly to judge that their own candidate was not really making inconsistent statements, while judging that the other guy was. More interesting—and potentially alarming—is what Westen learned from observing the participants' brains. It seemed that when viewing their own candidate's contradictory statements, the participants' brains initially registered neural activity indicating that they were experiencing conflict and discomfort. But they quickly compensated. In particular, the neural centers in charge of regulating emotional conflict "recruited" beliefs that allowed the participants to resolve what others would see as an obvious contradiction. And all this seemed to happen with very little involvement of the brain centers that are thought to be responsible for reasoning. And even more surprising, as the participants' found a way to get to their preferred conclusion, they not only began to experience less discomfort, but parts of the brain involved in positive emotions lit up, and they actually began to feel good. It was, Westen suggests, as if the brain was not only allowing bad reasoning, *it was actually rewarding it.*

These studies and others like them seem to undermine the role of reason: if we take their conclusion to the logical extreme, one begins to wonder about how important reasoning really is. If having reasons is not what causes you to make your political decisions, and my giving you reasons isn't going to change your mind, why bother with reasons in the first place?

Why not just bop you on the head, or manipulate you in some other way?

These are alarming questions, but they are premature, since studies of this sort don't in fact undermine the importance of reason, in particular the importance of the practices of reason that are basic to science. But they do give us some valuable insights into science's relation to other aspects of human psychology—in particular, emotion and intuition. This chapter examines these insights. As we shall see, they are interesting in their own right, but they are also useful in helping us to see what reason is and what it isn't.

## 2   Two Pictures

One obvious issue that the above examples highlight is how, and to what extent, our ability to reason is affected by emotion. Two competing images of the relation between emotion and reason have dominated Western philosophical thought. The first was given its most glorious rendition by Plato (something of a specialist in glorious images), who pictures reason as a charioteer, grappling to control the often conflicting and unruly winged horses of desire.[5] When things go well, the charioteer guides these horses with a steady hand. When things go poorly, the passions are given free rein, dragging us off to who knows where and leaving our bedraggled charioteer to make excuses in the morning.

The Hellenistic philosophers known as the Stoics refined this idea still further: to them, human emotions were simply irrational, and the best thing to do was to cut the horses loose from reason's chariot altogether. The key to happiness, the Stoics thought, was achieving *ataraxia* or an absence of disturbances of the soul. To achieve this state, we must purge ourselves of feelings—the "disturbances"—altogether. And not just the nasty disturbances, but the fun ones too, for plausibly enough, the Stoics thought you couldn't get rid of the one sort without getting rid of the other. Run into the hot embrace of Eros and you are in danger of the white-hot jealousy of Medea or the slow burn of Othello; pity the less fortunate and you might find that you end up, as Nietzsche predicted, despising them for their weakness.

Here's another way of thinking about it: in the Platonic/Stoic conception of human psychology, reason is the adult and emotion is the child. The adult either has to discipline the child strictly (Plato) or kick the little brat out of the house altogether (the Stoics). Either way, this basic picture of human reason has two components. The first is that emotion and reason are clearly separated—and frequently warring—sides of the human mind. And the second component is that, by and large, reason wins— at least in successful, happy people. Humans thus either are, or *ought* to be, chiefly rational animals.

Some ideas generate so much dust that they blanket almost everything. The traditional Platonic/Stoic conception of reason and emotion is like this. It covers everything from our worst gender stereotypes (men are rational and unfeeling, take-charge types while women are intuitive pseudo-children) to our pop-culture icons (*Star Trek*'s Mr. Spock has reason but no emotion, while his friend Bones seems the reverse). Perhaps most importantly, key elements of the Platonic conception of reason and emotion can be found among some of the basic operating assumptions of traditional economic theory: Standard economics assumes that our actions are the result of a detached, objective cost–benefit analysis on our own preferences. And there is no denying that this seems sensible in many cases. If I buy a book on Amazon, it must be because I wanted that book, and thought its cost was worth it. If the price of a commodity goes up to the point that its perceived value is outweighed by its cost, people buy less of it, and so on. In short, standard economics assumes that we are rational, that we can calculate the value of our options, that we learn from our mistakes, and that we do so without undue interference from emotions and other non-cognitive factors. The rational animal is the rational economic animal.

The Platonic picture of human reason and emotion, Father Reason and Child Feeling, is what Westen usefully calls the "dispassionate view of the human mind." The dispassionate view has been so influential in part because it resonates with some very common parts of human experience. We have all experienced saying or doing something (or both) that, in a later, cooler moment we regretted. Country music and the blues wouldn't have a subject matter if this wasn't the case—not to mention Greek tragedy. So passion frequently gets the better of us, and the very fact that we think of it this way suggests that, like Plato, we often think of emotions as something that should be controlled.

Yet the dispassionate view is pretty clearly at odds with other parts of human experience. Two considerations are particularly relevant. First, if, in order to be happy, we really must be guided only by the dispassionate charioteer of reason, we are out of luck. The average human being just isn't built like that. We are not dispassionate reasoners. People will vote for a candidate in a national election solely because of the candidate's stand on an issue the candidate has direct no control over even if elected—simply because that issue emotionally resonates with them.

(Thus, for instance, voters will support a candidate for local office because of his stance on whether a different state should allow same-sex couples to marry.) Businesses like Amazon.com have had enormous success offering *free* shipping on orders over a specified dollar amount. The result: people buy more just to get the free shipping—even when what they buy outweighs in cost what they save with the *free* shipping. And so on. As the behavioral economist Dan Ariely says, human beings are in fact *predictably* irrational in many situations—suggesting that some mistakes we make are not random errors but rooted much deeper in the average human makeup.[6] Since one ought to be only what one can be, and most folks don't seem to be able to be dispassionate reasoners, the Platonic command that they ought to be seems a moot point.

Even more problematic, however, is a second point: Not only are we not dispassionate reasoners, it would be very bad for us if we were. To some extent, this is also part of everyone's experience: most of us would agree that cold, uncaring people are not the sort we would want as a friend, a boss, or a lover. Indeed, far from thinking of dispassionate people as happy, most of us think of them as lonely and perhaps unhealthy.

But lacking emotion isn't just bad for our social life; it is bad because, as neurobiologist Antonio Damasio has famously argued, people lacking the capacity for certain types of emotions are severely impaired reasoners. Damasio's research indicates that one of the things that emotion does for us is to help provide "markers" or "internal guides."[7] Feelings, in other words, serve as indicators that allow us to connect ourselves in various ways with the circumstances in which we find ourselves. Without them, our ability to cope with those circumstances in a rational way drops. Damasio describes patients with damage to the frontal lobes, parts of the brain that are known to be involved in emotion and decision making, who had great difficulty making simple decisions like when to make an appointment. Without an emotional marker to guide them, they would methodically continue to weigh the utility of every option. Their practical reasoning, in short, was inhibited by their lack of emotion.

The most striking case of this sort is also the most famous patient in the neuroscience literature: Phineas Gage. Gage, a construction foreman in 1848, suffered an incredible accident: an explosion sent an iron bar through his skull. He was not killed, and indeed had a quick recovery. His knowledge and memory were not affected, but his emotional life was completely changed as a result of the accident. In particular, he no longer possessed any stable sense of what he cared about. Since he no longer seemed to have much feeling about any one thing more than another, he had a difficult time having any sort of enduring relationship or making plans. His ability to make reasonable choices dropped dramatically; his life, in short, came apart.

One of Damasio's many contributions to the literature is that he has documented a modern Phineas Gage—a patient he calls Elliot. Elliot has a benign brain tumor that affects the same area of the brain that was torn out by the bar that passed through Gage's skull. Like Gage, Elliot's emotional life was off-kilter or simply missing. He was cool and detached, seemingly caring about little. He performed quite well on IQ tests, and was good at calculations and discussing abstract topics. But he seemed, as Damasio remarks, to "approach life on a neutral note."[8] And like Gage, he couldn't make decisions, or life-plans, because he lacked any sort of emotional engagement. Without emotions to guide him, nothing seemed more worth doing than anything else.

As Damasio himself is concerned to emphasize, these examples suggest that emotions have an important part to play not just in life, but in our rational life, in our ability to reason about what to do and expect. How we feel about a situation can, as he puts it, "assist us with the daunting task of predicting an uncertain future and planning our actions accordingly."[9] Of course, those same feelings can distort our reactions and cause us to overestimate threats and underestimate problems. But as the cases of Gage and Elliot suggest, without them, our ability to solve practical decision-making problems is diminished or vanishes completely.

In the way I've been using the term, a reason is anything that explains why we ought to believe or do something. So in this sense feelings and emotional responses themselves can be reasons. Often they are bad reasons: one's envy of a colleague's success is not a good reason to speak ill of them. But sometimes they can be excellent reasons: my fondness for my child is an excellent reason for promoting her interests. And of course, like any reason, emotional reasons can also be overridden: my fondness for my daughter doesn't mean I should allow her to take other children's toys. This suggests that some emotions are not just "irrational" feelings, they contain cognitive elements that can be rationally assessed. Indeed, sometimes our feelings even provide us with reasons to do something that our upbringing and social views tell us we should not do. Mark Twain's *Huckleberry Finn* is an excellent example. At one point in the novel, Huck struggles with whether he should turn his friend Jim—a runaway slave—in to the authorities. Huck has been brought up to believe that slavery is morally acceptable, and that it is wrong for slaves to run away from their masters. These social norms are so ingrained into his worldview that they are part of his conscience. Nonetheless, Huck just can't bring himself to do what "he knows is right" because he feels overwhelmingly fond of Jim—Jim is his friend. As a result, Huck conceives of himself as a very bad and weak person—one who can't do as he morally ought to do. He feels guilty. What Huck doesn't realize (and the reader does) is that his feelings for Jim are excellent reasons to not turn Jim in. Indeed, his having those feelings tells us that Huck is more rational than the adults who have taught him that slavery is morally acceptable.[10]

So the Platonic conception of reason is a compelling but oversimplified picture. Human beings are not dispassionate reasoners, and it is a good thing too. This brings us to the other picture of reason's relation to emotion that I mentioned above. It is, in many ways, the exact opposite of the Platonic view. But as we'll see, it also shares with the Platonic view a crucial mistake.

## 3  Lifting a Finger

The most famous, and most brilliant, opponent of the Platonic picture of reason and emotion remains the eighteenth-century Scottish philosopher, David Hume. Hume's view was that humans are ruled not by reason but by what he called "passions" and "sentiment." Hume's expression of the point is characteristically vivid: "Reason is, and ought to be, the slave of the passions, and can never pretend to any other office than to serve and obey them."[11]

Hume's picture of how reason and emotion relate is the other influential idea I mentioned above. In one respect it is the exact opposite of the Platonic image. According to Hume, it is feelings, not reasons, that cause us to act. One way of putting this idea is that reason can only contribute to determining the means and not the ends of our actions. Reason can tell us "*If* you want *x*, then do *y*." But without passion, without desire, reason is simply inert. Reason and experience can give us information, tell us where we are on the map, so to speak. But reasons can't tell us where we want to go, or make us get up off the couch and head out the door. For that, we need a desire, a feeling or passion. We have to want it.

For Hume, reason's proper domain is mathematics and logic. He thought that these disciplines don't tell us about the world, however, but about the "relations between our ideas." Sense experience tells about the world around us—or at least purports to—but Hume infamously thinks that any inference we tend to make from this experience is apt to be rationally unjustified. Most such inferences—such as the supposition that the sun will rise tomorrow because it has every day in the past—are in fact, Hume thinks, the result of "custom and habit." And when it comes to deciding what we ought to do—to value judgments, in other words—reason's role is severely limited. Matters of value are matters of the heart.

Indeed, Hume sometimes seems to see our desires and passions as so immune from reason as to simply not be rationally evaluable. As he boldly puts it, "'Tis not contrary to reason to prefer the destruction of the whole world to the scratching of my finger. . . . 'Tis as little contrary to reason to prefer even my own acknowledged lesser good to my greater."[12] And, Hume adds, wanting something is neither rational nor irrational in itself. It just is. I either feel it or I don't. If I don't want to lift a finger to spare the world, then I may be cowardly, or malevolent, or depressed—but I am not, at least on that basis alone, irrational. I simply feel differently than most of us feel. The trick, therefore, is not to get me to see the light of reason, but to get me to stop feeling the way I do—or better put, to get me to *start* feeling, to start caring about everyone else.

The full range of Hume's writings on these topics is wide, and the details complex and up for dispute. Nonetheless, the picture I've painted so far, even in such broad strokes, is generally understood as Hum*ean*, whether or not it was Hume's actual considered view. That picture flips the Platonic image upside down: in the Humean picture, emotion's on top and reason's on the bottom. It's passion, not reason, that causes us to act, and the emotional aspects of our lives—feelings, desires, and so on—are immune to rational assessment. Emotion brooks no lip, so to speak, from its slave.

Even so roughly described, it is clear that the Humean picture has charms its stiffer, Platonic rival lacks. It is earthier. And as such, it seems more in line with the way people actually are. It is a measure of Hume's influence on contemporary intellectual culture that we now find his views about emotion and reason so natural. But as we saw with the Platonic picture of reason and emotion, we must guard against taking it to extremes.

Consider the idea that emotions can't be rationally assessed. Unless it is significantly qualified, this is very implausible. Imagine you accidentally spill some wine on your dinner partner's shirtsleeve. Suppose he shouts at you, stands up, and storms out. This would be inappropriate, to put it mildly. And note: it is not just the behavior that is inappropriate—so is the anger it expresses. Mild annoyance is justified in such a situation; extreme anger is not. And it wouldn't make any more sense (indeed, its creepiness factor would increase) if he simply seethed about it privately. The anger itself, and not just its expression, is inappropriate given the circumstances. As we might put it: your dinner partner had *no reason* to be so angry.

The fact that we use words like "inappropriate" and "sense-less" with regard to feelings, while taking other feelings to be apt (such as grief at the death of a loved one), indicates that the matter is more complicated than an unqualified Humean picture can make it seem. One complication is that when we talk about "emotions" we are really talking about a large range of mental states. On the one hand are those that seem simplest and are arguably universal: fear, happiness, anger, sadness, surprise, and disgust are the usual examples.[13] These sorts of emotions seem characterized by what some psychologists call "affect programs"— widely shared responses due to mechanisms that are not within conscious control. But sometimes when we are talking about emotions we are talking about very complex states: resentment is one example; regret is another. These states often seem built out of multiple components—affective and cognitive components.

Most of us would agree with Hume that emotions are passive and not under the control of our will. But it still seems that we do evaluate them, and indeed we sometimes hold people responsible for having them.[14] The angry dinner partner, again, can be criticized: it didn't make sense for him to be so angry at such a trivial, unintentional act. (Of course, if the wine-spilling was part of a long-term plan of harassment, that's a different story.) Moreover, you will hold him responsible for his boorishness; one doubts further dinner invitations will be on the way.[15]

We can say all these things and still acknowledge what is right about the Humean picture. All motivations may have an emotional component, but that needn't leave our ability to make rational inferences, and form beliefs on the evidence without a significant role to play. It is one thing to claim, plausibly enough, that emotions are always involved in any practical judgment; it is another to claim, implausibly, that reason is never involved.

We can even grant Hume's idea that our passions give us our ends—they tell us what matters to us—while reason tells us the means to those ends. But acknowledging either point hardly means we have to think that our ends can't be criticized. Someone, for example, who is indifferent to someone else's suffering can be criticized precisely because of this indifference. Some things that people want are desires without any justification—even if, sadly, they don't (or even can't) recognize that fact. In short, we can acknowledge emotion's central and powerful role in our decision-making but still concede that what actually motivates someone to do something may not be what *should* motivate them, and vice versa. Moreover, in order to be able to acknowledge this humble truth, we don't need to appeal to the idea that there are acts we should be motivated to do simply by virtue of our cold-hearted appreciation of the facts— by Platonic-style Reason alone.[16] Perhaps there are such acts, the product of a super-faculty capable of producing reasons that have authority for us independently of our psychologies. But nothing I've said so far forces you to think so, nor will I try to convince you otherwise.

Like mirror-images of one another, the archetypical Platonic and Humean pictures of the relation between reason and emotion have opposite orientations. But they have a common flaw. They treat reason and emotion as more independent than they seem likely to be. The Platonic conception wrongly imagines that we can do without emotion (and will be better reasoners, and better people for it); the unqualified Humean conception holds that emotions can't be assessed rationally. The truth is likely to be messier: neither reason nor emotion is the master or slave; they intertwine more intimately and equally than that.

## 4 Intuition: What Just Seems Right

Some people have an amazing ability to look at a particular sort of problem and know what the solution is. There are people who can put together or take apart very complicated machinery without ever having to look at the directions or even (seemingly) pause for thought. And I've known other people who can "see" solutions to mathematical or logical problems faster than others can sit down and work them out. And most of us, psychologists tell us, have some degree of emotional intuition—the ability of to instantly read from their faces what other people are feeling. Human beings, as we put it, are intuitive.

I opened this chapter by noting two experiments. One—the study about political partisans and brain activity—led us into a discussion of the relation between emotion and reason. But the first experiment I mentioned—about the unnerving correlation between snap judgments of "competence" and the outcome of elections—actually raises another issue, interconnected with the first: that of the relation between intuition and reason. In particular, it raises the issue of the relative reliability of thinking things through versus making intuitive or unreflective judgments.

Many philosophers, such as Kant and Henri Bergson, have thought that intuition is a single special way of learning about the world. Intuitions, on this view, are like perceptions into the nature of things. This is most plausible in the case of mathematical or logical intuition, such as the intuition that 2 and 2 make 4. Such propositions just seem to be true, "we see" that they are.

But there are least two reasons not to take the analogy with perception too seriously. The first is that a special sort of perception suggests a special sort of organ that has evolved to engage in it; and there is no evidence that we have any such organ of intuition. (Which is not to deny of course, that there may be evolutionary explanations for why we have intuitions. It is just that these explanations seem unlikely to appeal to a single and biologically unified *perceptual* system directly analogous to, e.g., the visual system.) So while it is an evocative metaphor, it is misleading to think of "intuition" as *literally* a type of special sight—the inner eye of the mind, so to speak. The second reason is that the variety of propositions and thoughts we can find intuitive (from propositions about sets to whether someone we meet is attracted to us) is far too wide to form one distinct module. Intuition is a wide-ranging phenomenon, incorporating both snap visual judgments and mathematical insight.

So if asked to define "intuition" in general, I think the best we can say is this: *When we intuit something, we find it believable without knowing why.*[17] This definition links intuition to belief without defining the one as the other: to intuit something is to find it *believable,* even if we don't always end up believing what we intuit.[18] But we don't find it believable because of the explicit evidence we've seen in favor of an idea. Intuitions are "source-opaque." We don't know what causes us to find the proposition believable. Our finding it so doesn't *seem* to be due to our specific perceptions, or to memory, testimony, or any of the usual sources of evidence. As the psychologist Jonathan Haidt puts it, intuitive judgments are marked by the fact that they appear "suddenly and effortlessly in consciousness, without any awareness by the person of the mental processes that led to the outcome."[19] This seems right. In Thomas Hoving's interesting study of fake artworks, Hoving invokes the infamous fakebuster and early twentieth century art historian Bernard Berenson:

[He] sometimes distressed his colleagues with his inability to articulate how he could see so clearly the tiny defects and inconsistencies in a particular work that branded it either an unintelligent reworking or a fake. In one court case, in fact, Berenson was able to say only that his stomach felt wrong.[20]

Examples like the fakebuster suggest an interesting possibility. When we conceive of ourselves as intuiting something, the causes of the judgment in question are unknown to us. But those causes are likely due to *a complex interaction of more usual sources of evidence*, sources like visual experience and memory. Art experts have become experts because they've seen lots of art, and because they are good at detecting patterns, remembering details, and noting connections between art objects. But much of that information—like so much of the information any of us uses—gets stored far deeper in the shelves of the brain than is usually accessible to consciousness. Expertise is something that develops over time due to the formation of a huge amount of what Michael Polyani called *tacit knowledge* about a subject matter.[21] The expert can make intuitive judgments in her area of expertise without having any theory (or even caring to have a theory) about how she does it. She just "sees how it is," and not because of any occult power, but because she has assembled a huge amount of tacit knowledge. Indeed, all of us have a lot of tacit knowledge, even about things we aren't "experts" in. Chomsky and others have argued for decades that that our knowledge of grammar is largely tacit. We all employ grammatical rules without being able to explicitly articulate them or even understand their empirical consequences. We employ them intuitively.

So intuition is not mysterious or occult. It probably isn't even a unified phenomenon. The only thing in common between all the things that we call "intuitions" is that each of them is something we find believable without knowing why. And of course, that means that you might intuit what I do not. I might not find what you intuit to be believable, or I might find it believable but know why I do so—I might, for example, know quite a bit about the rules of grammar. Intuition is not occult, but it is a personal matter.

Like emotion, intuition is not separate from or independent of reason. Several points suggest this. One is that if the above analysis of intuition is right, much of our intuition could in fact be, unbeknownst to the person doing the intuiting, the product of sources that are also available to reflective, conscious processing: induction from experience; observation; deduction. These sources, when applied consciously, are paradigmatic of reason. If so, then the fact that the causal basis of intuitive judgments happens behind the scenes doesn't necessarily mean that this basis is nonrational. To think otherwise would require buying at least two dubious assumptions: that rational cognition is *necessarily* conscious, and that the causal basis of intuitive judgments is *necessarily* unavailable to reflection. Neither assumption seems warranted. As I have already indicated, judgments that some people make intuitively—about grammar, or about whether an artwork is a fake, or about the truth of a mathematical proposition—can also be made through deliberation, by consciously applying certain rules, for example. But that just shows what everyone knows: some people can believe things by intuition that others can't. Nor does it seem warranted to hold that rational thought is essentially conscious. It is true that most of the justifications and explanations we are interested in are those that we can access by conscious reflection. But why not think that sometimes the process of explanation and justification happens beneath the level of immediate attention? If so, then the products of that process could still sometimes qualify, in the above minimal sense, as intuitions.

Moreover, our intuitions, just like our emotional experiences, can be rationally assessed—in particular, they can be judged as coherent or incoherent with our other beliefs and intuitions. For example, I have the intuition that no proposition can be both true and false. But then what do I say of the proposition *This proposition is false*? It appears to be true if false and false if true. Paradoxes like this show that our intuitions can conflict, and when they do so, we look to reconcile them, to make them more coherent. This is most striking in the case of moral dilemmas. Suppose you could save ten innocent people from certain death (an evildoer will shoot them) by killing a single innocent person. Would you do it? Most folks, whatever their eventual answer, feel a conflict of intuitions. It feels wrong to kill an innocent person; but it also feels wrong to allow ten people to be killed when you can stop it. Confronted with cases like this, most folks feel an overwhelming temptation to ask questions about the hypothetical setup: Do we really know for sure that the evildoer will keep his word to spare the ten if you kill the one? Are the people in question really innocent?—and so on. The temptation to ask such questions makes sense—it as an attempt to find some point where our reason can get its grip on the case, some difference that

will allow us to reach a principled answer, to genuinely
resolve the conflict of intuitions. As even the psychologist
Jonathan Haidt—no friend of the role of reason in moral
judgment—recognizes, reason plays a role in reconciling competing intuitions.[22]

In sum, intuition is not entirely independent of reason. Intuitions might themselves be the products of some of the paradigmatic sources of rational beliefs, and intuitions themselves can
be assessed as for rational coherence. This is why Todorov's and
similar studies, while obviously important, do not undermine
the role of reason. What they show is that many people may
make their decisions about who to vote for based on factors that
can be assessed extremely quickly by visual intake. Perhaps there
is a type of cognitive heuristic at work—a shortcut of sorts,
which allows human beings to make high-speed assessments of
other humans. Even if there is, however, that doesn't mean (nor
does Todorov himself suggest) that people who have already
decided to vote against someone because of their policies will
necessarily be swayed by seeing their face—although of course,
they might be (hence the political meet and greet). Nor does it
entail that people's judgments about that subsequent independent information (for example, about a candidate's voting
record on matters the voter cares about) won't have any effect
on their decisions in the voting booth.

In short, the mere fact that many of our decisions—including
our decisions about value—are being made by "a ubiquitous and
under-studied intuitive process" doesn't mean that reason plays
no role in those decisions.[23] The fact that reason has a significant role to play in judgment doesn't mean that we must see it
as the single star of the show; it shares the stage with intuition
as well as emotion.

## 5 Without Reason?

So defending reason doesn't mean defending the idea that we are dispassionate, unintuitive robots. This shouldn't be too surprising if we remember that by "reason" I mean our capacity to explain and justify, and more narrowly, our capacity to justify by appeal to some very basic methods of belief: observation and logical inference. This conception of reason is neutral. It doesn't require that "reason" is always the captain of our mental chariot. Nor, as I've indicated, does it mean that reason can't evaluate the emotions. If to reason is to engage in justification, and there can be unjustified and justified emotions and intuitions, then emotions and intuitions can be rationally evaluated. Moreover, this idea stakes nothing on the thought that only humans have the capacity to give and ask for reasons. Perhaps other animals have it too; that is a scientific question well beyond the bounds of this book.

But simply defining reason in this straightforward way doesn't get us completely out of the woods. For even if conceiving of each other as justifiers or reason-givers doesn't mean we must be dispassionate reason-givers, you might still think that *scientific* reasoning is toothless when it really counts. By "scientific" reasons, I mean reasons in what I earlier called the narrower sense of the term: appeals to evidence generated by the methods employed in scientific practice. Doesn't the evidence suggest that *these* sorts of reasons are irrelevant to people's judgments in real life? Perhaps, as Westen puts it, "the political brain is an emotional brain."[24]

In another study, Westen presented shoppers in a mall with a fake news story about Abu Ghraib.[25] The story was close in detail to actual stories then appearing in the press. It detailed how a U.S. soldier was on trial before a military judge for the torture of Iraqi prisoners. The soldier's defense was that his superiors had led him to believe that the rules relating to torturing prisoners had changed. Westen and his researchers gave their subjects five different versions of the story, each of which varied in how much evidence the soldier had to back it up (from none at all to some corroborating testimony to smoking-gun memos). The subjects were then given a questionnaire that asked for their feelings about the U.S. military and human rights, and then asked them whether they believed this soldier had a case. The results again were striking: given a subject's responses to the questions about their feelings toward the military and human rights, together with the amount of evidence they had been given, the researchers could predict that subject's judgment 84.5 percent of the time. But given just their "emotional" responses to questions about the military and human rights, they *could still predict the judgments 84 percent of the time.* In short, the amount of evidence a subject was given seemed to have little effect on their eventual judgment.

Westen himself wishes to draw two lessons from this. One is political. He thinks that American conservatives have long understood that humans are ruled by passion and not reason. Liberals, on the other hand, have an "irrational emotional commitment to rationality"—a commitment they had best abandon if they want to start winning back the electorate. More broadly, Westen thinks that if politicians of any stripe are going to sway the electorate, they've got to do so with emotional, not intellectual appeals. Whether this is correct depends on which aspect of Westen's message is in question. It is certainly the case that emotion is a major player in political decision-making, but this isn't something we need a brain scientist to tell us. The ancient

Greek Sophists, proponents of what we still call "rhetoric," were experts at advising politicians on how to win arguments by, among other things, appealing to emotions. And politicians have found that technique effective ever since (while political consultants continue to find that coaching them on how to do it is a very lucrative business).

Westen's second, and more interesting, suggestion brings us back to the worry with which we began this section. As he puts it: "when the outcomes of a political decision have strong emotional implications, and the data leave even the slightest room for artistic license, reason plays virtually no role in the decision-making process."[26] In other words: when it *comes to political and value judgments*, epistemic reasons aren't causally efficacious.

No doubt this is true in many particular cases. But it is dangerous to overgeneralize. To see why, return to the study about people's reactions to torture at Abu Ghraib. Its results are striking. But notice how Westen interprets the data: he claims that it shows that people's judgments are the result of emotional factors and not of the information they've been given. But there is another possible interpretation of these results, one implied by a well-known theory of judgment referred to as the Quine–Duhem hypothesis. It goes like this: our beliefs form a web or lattice-like structure. Like the strands of a web, our beliefs are connected. Some of your beliefs are at the edge of the web—change one of those, and the structure of your web of belief changes only slightly. But some of your beliefs are like the dense strands at the center of a web—change one of these, and the whole web changes. So it is not surprising that human beings are very reluctant to change those core beliefs. Most of us are by nature conservative reasoners; if new experience comes along that seems to challenge one of our core commitments, our first reaction won't be to give up that core commitment. Our first reaction will be to question the experience and new information, or to alter *other of our beliefs* so that we can retain the more central ones. As Quine famously noted: "there is much latitude of choice as to what statement to reevaluate in the light of any single contrary experience."[27] That is, there is *always* "room for artistic license" (as Westen puts it). The facts by themselves can never force us to see things just one way: "Any statement can be held true come what may, if we make drastic enough adjustments elsewhere in the system."[28]

The Quine–Duhem hypothesis predicts that this is just an extreme example of how all of us reason all the time. Indeed, as Thomas Kuhn famously argued in the 1960s, this is precisely what happens in science as well. Scientists, no less than the rest of us, have certain theoretical commitments that they would die in a ditch over. These are the commitments that form the core of a modern scientific paradigm. It takes a lot of inconsistent information for us to change our minds about such commitments; we are prone to alter our views about other matters so as to "shield" our core beliefs from criticism. This means that there is another way to interpret Westen's results. Again, Westen takes his study to show that increased information doesn't change our minds in the face of an *emotional* attachment to one side of an issue. But the Quine–Duhem hypothesis suggests a simpler explanation: *it is just very difficult to change people's minds about their core beliefs and commitments—about those that sit near the center of their worldview.* What Westen's study suggests isn't a dramatic clash between emotion and reason. It is a more humdrum clash between our prior, deep-seated commitments and new data that seemingly conflicts with those commitments. If it is (somehow) a central part of your worldview that the

United States doesn't torture prisoners, then it should not be surprising that a single news story will not convince you otherwise. To change our core commitments takes an enormous amount of challenging information. What the Quine–Duhem analysis shows is that this is not surprising. *This is how rational deliberation and judgment work*, and not only in science (which is what Duhem and Quine were interested in) but in daily life. Thus, the fact of our recalcitrance in the face of new information is not a sign that reason doesn't matter. It simply illustrates that reason often works slowly.

Even if the Quine–Duhem hypothesis can explain why we might be reluctant to change our beliefs in the face of new data, you might think it still leaves a basic objection standing to the idea that reasons in the narrower sense play any causal role in our decision making about value. There is considerable data suggesting that much reasoning about value is post hoc. We judge intuitively first and then make up explanations later. And this fact, you might think, is entirely compatible with our making decisions within a web of belief. Indeed, we might often simply judge intuitively that some information is incompatible with our beliefs and only later claim that there are principled reasons (beyond those of consistency) to not revise our system. Perhaps, as the well-known psychologist Jonathan Haidt says, we are caught in a "wag-the-dog" illusion, thinking that reason is the tail that wags the dog of moral judgment.[29]

I have two comments on this. The first is that, as I'll indicate again below, this point, if it is correct, applies far more widely than to moral judgments. The scope of the Quine–Duhem hypothesis, as I've already indicated, is wide: it applies to cognition in general. So the threat of post-hoc reasoning is always with us (as we all readily know, on reflection).

The more important point is this: the wag-the-dog view holds that reasons *only or mostly* play a post-hoc role in value judgments. But this is inconsistent with what seems to be an obvious fact: people *do* change their core commitments, even those to which they are emotionally and intuitively attached. Moreover, some of these changes appear to happen because of an appreciation of new reasons and data.

Here's one example: Americans' shifting attitudes toward race. While not changing as much as we would like, there is no question that over the last century, many Americans came to change their minds on a number of issues concerning race, and in particular, about the fairness of openly discriminatory practices and laws. One common explanation for these changes appeals to changes in attitude that result from what is perceived as a "group threat." According to this idea, members of a dominant group are more prone to endorse and engage in openly discriminatory behavior given a perception of threat from members of less dominant groups. But while group-threat phenomena seem to play a role in changing views about discrimination, many researchers now see it as an incomplete explanation at best. One reason is that group-threat theories imply that attitudes toward antiblack discrimination within a population, for example, will co-vary across time in relation to the percentage of blacks within that population. But the black percentage of the population in the U.S. varied only slightly from 1972 to 1991, yet views about discrimination toward blacks changed significantly during those years. Consequently, the percentage of blacks within a population is not itself a possible explanation of attitudes toward discrimination.[30] So what is the explanation? Well, clearly there is not just one. Factors that need to be considered are the impact of historical events and the interaction of implicitly prejudicial attitudes with other elements of personal psychology. But several researchers have argued that intellectual developments constitute another causal factor. Just one example of such a development is the increasingly widespread acceptance, among mid-twentieth-century Americans, of the idea that much behavior is due to cultural and environmental factors and not just heredity. In turn, this encourages the thought that differences between individuals and groups of individuals are often due to contingent factors. This idea spread in part because social scientists raised it, and the data that supported it, in college courses. And "this suggests that the effect of education changed over birth cohorts as the social sciences became more prominent in universities, as happened after World War II."[31] If so, then it seems reasonable that views about the relative importance of environmental influence can be seen as at least one part of the explanation for changes in attitudes toward discriminatory practice. And that in turn suggests that the spread of scientific knowledge can make a difference.

If that is so, then we have an example of how intellectual positions, supported by the results of scientific work, can have an indirect (but still important) causal effect on politically relevant behavior. Indeed, this seems to be just one example. Many Americans' attitudes toward environmental conservation, the Iraq war, and climate change, to cite a few other examples, have changed over time. Such glacial shifts in viewpoint about core political issues cannot be simply attributed to either "reason" or emotion." Both presumably play a role—and that is of course the point. Changes in people's attitudes, even attitudes about value, are sometimes due, at least in part, to the influence of scientific reasons. This is why scientific education clearly matters so much to the development of a healthy democracy: it has played a historical role in identifying prejudice and bias.

And it is just as implausible to suggest that such explanations are all post hoc rationalizations. Indeed, it is difficult to see why views like Haidt's and Westen's aren't self-defeating. The judgment that reasons play no role in judgment is itself a judgment. And Westen has defended it with reasons. So if those reasons persuade me his theory is true, then reasons can play a role in judgment—and his theory is false.

You might respond by saying that the reasons to accept views like Haidt's and Westen's are not value judgments. They are scientific claims. But even the most "scientific" of claims is *informed* by value judgments. Science itself presupposes certain values: truth, objectivity, and what I called "epistemic principles" in chapter 1. Epistemic principles are principles that tell us what is rational or right to believe. They include, at the most fundamental level, principles about which methods and sources of belief I should trust. So epistemic principles are normative; they are values. Most of the time, we take our epistemic principles as obvious, and so assume that they are not in play. But that doesn't mean they aren't. When making a judgment about the age of the earth or the biological development of humans, I am making a judgment that takes for granted certain standards of evidence—standards I usually take you, my interlocutor, to share. And I may only come to realize that these are values when you disagree with me—when you point out that I am assuming that certain types of evidence (say, evidence culled from a lab) are more valuable than others (say, what is written in the Bible).

Indeed, nothing we do is completely free of value judgments. As Todorov's clever experiment indicates, even our split-second perceptions seem to come preloaded with values—we can and often do judge someone to be trustworthy or competent, suspicious, or inept on sight. Again, this isn't necessarily something we need elaborate studies to tell us: even if they aren't very good at spotting prejudice in themselves, most folks are aware of how prejudice and preconception can stain judgments about anything from who deserves the biggest raise (the white man or the black woman?) to who is the best candidate for president (the liberal or the conservative?). Again, even in science, judgments—and hence, values—come into play. Outside of mathematics (and sometimes even there) it is rare that the data is so conclusive that there is just one conclusion we can draw. Usually the data admits of more than one interpretation, more than one explanation. And that means that we must infer, or judge what we think is the case. And where there is judgment, there are values in the background.

The lesson here is that if reason has no role in value judgments, it will have little role in any judgment, including this one. But rather than embrace this conclusion, it seems more sensible to admit that reason can play a role in our judgments—perhaps not the role that Plato would have wanted, one completely free of emotion, but a role nonetheless.

A final point. Even if the foregoing is incorrect—even if, in other words, reason really does have *no* role in political judgments—it would still have value. The very act of giving and asking for reasons has tremendous political importance. This is because it is part of what we mean by a democratic state that, at least in theory, such states are governed by reason. In a democracy, disagreements between citizens are to be handled in the arena of reason alone, and arguments that legitimate the various uses of political power by citizens and the state must be backed by reasons. And crucially, the reasons in question cannot be reasons of force or manipulation. Beating a person up is a very easy way to "convince" them; fear and pain are tried and true motivators. But these are not the sorts of "reasons" that can be counted as legitimate in a democracy. I cannot justify my political claims to you by simply wielding power over you, for so doing violates the fundamental liberal democratic principle that I treat you with equal respect. Rather, I must try to persuade you that my view of the facts is closer to the truth than your own. Only then do I treat you as an autonomous, rational being who is capable of judging on her own what to believe.

# 3 "Nothing but Dreams and Smoke"

## 1 Skepticism from the Tower

It is one of the little ironies of history that skepticism is rarely more popular than with true believers. The theological disputes at the heart of the sixteenth-century Protestant Reformation are a case in point. People were killing each other over who had the best method to access religious truth. Protestants claimed the best method was personal meditation on scripture; Catholics retorted that it was obedience to clergy and tradition. During the course of this dispute, the rediscovered writings of an obscure ancient Roman writer, Sextus Empiricus, dropped like a bomb.[1]

Sextus's *Outlines of Pyrrhonism* hardly has "literary fame" written all over it. It is dense and difficult to read, and doesn't even purport to be all that original—Sextus claims, rather, to give a sort of CliffsNotes for the (now-lost) writings of Greek skeptics. But it contained something of real interest to Protestant and Catholic theologians trying to defend their own standard of religious truth: an intellectual weapon.

The weapon in question is a very simple argument—due originally, perhaps, to the Greek philosopher Agrippa. It is sometimes called Agrippa's "tri-lemma," and it goes like this: Every belief is produced by some method or source, be it humble (like memory) or complex (like technologically assisted science). But why think those methods are trustworthy or reliable? If I challenge one of your methods, you can't just appeal to the same method to show that it is reliable. That would be circular. And appealing to another method won't help either—for unless *that* method can be shown to be reliable, using it to determine the reliability of the first method answers nothing. So you end up either continuing on in the same vein—pointlessly citing reasons for methods and methods for reasons forever—or arguing in circles, or granting that your method is groundless. Any way you go, it seems you must admit you can give no reason for trusting your methods, and hence can give no reason to believe.

To the theologians on both sides of the Reformation's wars, this argument was like a gift from heaven. Here at last was a way of demolishing the enemy's principles! The Protestant theologian could ask: How do you *know* that consulting Church authorities is a guide to truth? If the Catholics replied that they knew because the Church said so then they were arguing in a circle; but if they cited the Bible, they were abandoning their method for another. Unfortunately for Protestant theologians, the Catholics could and did use the same argument. They asked: How do you *know* that personal reflection on scripture is a guide to truth? If the Protestant replied that meditating on scripture had revealed it to be, then he was guilty of circular reasoning; but if he appealed to some other authority, then he had admitted that his scriptural method was not the final word.[2]

As always happens with so-called miracle weapons, this one settled nothing. The upshot was that neither side seemed capable of defending its standard of religious truth without assuming it—which, of course, had been Sextus's point. According to Sextus, what his argument showed was that we should just stop believing anything—never claim anything is true, religious or otherwise. Needless to say, this was not a popular conclusion among theologians on either side of the Reformation. Not-believing is not an option for the militant believer. So many of them just kept Sextus's arguments but rejected his conclusion. If reason can't show that your method of belief is the right one, then don't give up on the method, give up on reason.

Religious debates were by no means the only symptom of the sweeping intellectual changes happening around this time. Already by the sixteenth century, Copernican ideas, though not yet verified by Galileo, were seeding a revolution in cosmology, and some had already begun to doubt that the earth was, as the Church had long taught, the center of the universe. Moreover, it was clear that Europeans had even been wrong about geography—new lands were being discovered, inhabited by new peoples (think: "Intelligent Life Discovered on the Moon!"). In each case, debates over the facts led quickly into debates over how to know the facts. Which was the best method for knowing about the structure of the universe (observation and induction or Church authority)? Which was the best method for determining the shape of the earth (charting by ship or using ancient Greek mathematical models)? And this meant that not only were the facts disputed, but there were live disagreements over who had the right standards for knowledge.

It is worth pausing for a moment to think about the impact all these disagreements would have on a thoughtful person living at the time. To get yourself in the right frame of mind, imagine that you woke up one day to these headlines:

EXPERTS DECLARE: EARTH REALLY CENTER OF UNIVERSE!

This would turn your life upside down. You no doubt wouldn't believe it at first. After all, if it were true, then almost everything you thought you knew about the universe would have been a mistake. If the earth is absolutely fixed in space and something as gigantic as the sun revolves around that absolute point, then, just for starters, we are wrong about gravity. Maybe there is no gravity—no force, in other words, that is a function of mass. Or maybe the sun is just much, much smaller—and maybe the stars are the size they appear to be in the night sky. Either way, all modern astronomy, all physics would have to go. We'd be starting over. The mind boggles.

When this sort of sudden upheaval really happens, doubting authority is a natural response. If the experts suddenly declared that all of modern physics had been a mistake, you might eventually believe it. Or you might just decide that the experts aren't really experts after all—perhaps their methods are simply bad methods. Indeed, you might reject the whole idea of "expertise" and "method" in physics as a scam. You might begin to suspect we have no reason to believe anything.

If you were an intellectual in the sixteenth century, this is just the situation you would have been in. One such intellectual was Michel de Montaigne (1533–1592). Montaigne was a philosopher, a political player, and a brilliant essayist (he invented the essay, in fact). He was also smitten with Sextus—so much so that he had some of the Roman's sayings carved into the beams of his study. He took Sextus's skepticism about reason to provide an antidote to the religious zealotry of his day. Yet like others in his day, Montaigne didn't think that the right solution was to give up on religious belief. Rather, what we learn from Sextus, Montaigne argued, is that "Man's plague is the belief that he has knowledge. That is why ignorance is so highly recommended by our religion as appropriate for belief and obedience."[3] It wasn't just the experts that were to blame. Human reason itself, Montaigne insisted, was stained and flawed; it could not be trusted. Reason was like a serpent eating its tail: "For those who argue by presuppositions, one must suppose, on the contrary, the very axiom about which one is arguing." Consequently, we need to put our trust in something else: we need to trust the faith we were born into. "There cannot be any principles for men, unless the Divinity has revealed those principles to them," he wrote. "All the rest . . . is nothing but dreams and smoke."[4]

The reception of Sextus's argument in the sixteenth century and Montaigne's ensuing popularization of it supply us with at least two take-home lessons. The first is that skepticism about reason finds its most receptive audience in uncertain times, when there is disagreement over not just the facts, but over the best method for knowing the facts. The second is linked to the first. The importance of Sextus's argument, and the importance of answering it, stems from its obvious consequence—one that Montaigne, with characteristic adroitness, put his finger on. If I can't give reasons for why I think my methods are reliable, then it is not clear how my commitment to those methods can be understood as rational. And that, in turn, raises the question of how even changing your mind about which methods to trust can be a rational process, as opposed to something more like a religious conversion.

## 2  Certain and Assured

Sometime near the end of 1628, a number of the leading intellectuals of the day gathered in Paris at the home of the papal nuncio. The occasion was a speech by a rather odd and ambitious chemist by the name of Chandoux, whose expertise was in base metals—and who, incidentally, was later hanged for counterfeiting coins. It must have been quite a scene: The audience included the celebrated philosopher Marin Mersenne and one of the eminent thinkers of the Counter Reformation, Cardinal Pierre Bérulle. Chandoux's speech was fashionably skeptical; he denounced Aristotelian philosophy and suggested that knowledge might be found in probabilities. He was applauded by all in attendance, save for a rather spare fellow in his thirties, who, invited by Bérulle, rose to offer an impassioned reply.[5] It was right, the man said, to renounce the failed Scholastic methods of the schools; but it would be a grave mistake to allow themselves to be "dupes of probabilities." The new science could never be defended by ceding ground to the skeptics. The key was rather to find a new method, what he called the *Méthod naturelle*, which would, he thought, determine something "so certain and so assured that all the most extravagant suppositions brought forward by the skeptics were incapable of shaking it."[6]

The speaker was René Descartes. He was thirty-two at the time, and already responsible for laying the foundations of analytical geometry. We do not know in detail what he said that day, but it must have been impressive. Bérulle took him aside afterward and urged Descartes to apply himself full-time to philosophy. It was fateful advice.

Descartes lived a generation after Montaigne. A great mathematician, he was gripped by the same problems and dismayed by the same disagreements over method that had so unsettled his predecessor. Like Montaigne, Descartes had been schooled in the medieval Scholastic tradition, a tradition that, even with regard to secular questions, generally taught that the answers were to be gained by consulting authorities—principally Aristotle. And again like Montaigne, Descartes had come to see Aristotelian principles as mistaken. His most famous work starts with the following words: "Some years ago I was struck by the large number of falsehoods that I had accepted as true in my childhood, and the highly doubtful nature of the whole edifice that I had subsequently based upon them."[7] In short, Descartes had come to reject his earlier first principles—including, it turns out, his epistemic first principles, those that told him what was rational and what wasn't. But where Montaigne thought it was folly to try and find a reason for adopting some first principles over others, Descartes's goal was to do just that: to come up with a method that would provide a firm foundation for the emerging new science. This was a theoretical quest, but in Descartes's day it must have been pregnant with practical meaning. For if foundational principles existed, appealing to them could not only determine whose methods were the right ones, it could show why changing your mind about such matters wasn't like religious conversion. It would show—to ourselves and others—that we can give reasons for trusting reason.

Descartes's idea was to start with what is so "clear and distinct" that it is immune to doubt. This last part is crucial: according to Descartes, in order to find out what is true, you should first subject your beliefs to doubt—play the skeptic, as it were, with yourself. Reject all those beliefs you can doubt even a little, and what's left will be what is absolutely certain—the stones upon which you can rebuild your knowledge. There weren't many stones in the yard, as it turned out. Descartes thought we could doubt almost everything we believe, including that there is a physical world around us, since it is possible that an evil demon is generating a massive and constant illusion for our benefit. Perhaps this demon is making me believe that I am here at my desk in my house writing these words, when in reality I am doing no such thing. Perhaps the external world—along with my desk, my house, these words—is an illusion. So what *is* immune from this sort of total doubt? Consider the thought that you are thinking right now. No matter how skeptical you force yourself to be—or I force myself to be—we can't doubt we are thinking right now, because doubting *is* thinking. I can doubt that you think, and vice versa, of course. But the proposition that I am thinking right now is properly self-evident—*clear and distinct*—for everyone who thinks it.

So the foundation of knowledge, for Descartes, is our privileged access to the contents of our own minds. But how were we to get past that limited starting point? Descartes needed a theoretical bridge—one that would get us from the island of our mental life to the wider shores of the world. He looked within himself and found an idea of perfection. This idea (like any other) must have a cause. But causes, Descartes argued, must have at least as much reality as their effects. So if anything causes the idea of perfection, it must itself be something perfect. In short: we do have the idea of perfection, something perfect must have caused it, and so a perfect being—God—must exist. And if he exists, and is perfect, then he would not deceive us. So what is clearly and distinctly perceived must really be true. Knowledge is secured.

Descartes's gambit to move knowledge beyond the borders of the mind hasn't proven very convincing. The problem here is not just that Descartes appeals to something equally contro-versial (the existence of God) to solve skepticism. Nor just that it rests on some dubious assumptions (why think an idea of perfection must itself be perfect?). The real problem is that it is not clear how this move could have succeeded in the first place. Descartes was certain that there must be a God because he had a clear and distinct proof that God existed; but he thinks that clear and distinct ideas must be true because there is a God. This is the so-called Cartesian Circle, and it is just the sort of cir-cularity that Sextus's argument predicts we will always get into when trying to defend our basic epistemic principles.[8] As Hume, himself a fan of Sextus and Montaigne, would later put it:

[Descartes] recommends an universal doubt, not only of all of our former opinions and principles, but also of our very faculties, of whose veracity, say they, we must assure ourselves, by a chain of reasoning, deduced from some original principle, which cannot possibly be falla-cious or deceitful. But neither is there any such original principle, which has a prerogative above others, that are self-evident and con-vincing: Or if there were, could we advance a step beyond it, but by the use of those very faculties, of which we are supposed to be already diffident.[9]

Hume elegantly sums up the basic problem with Descartes's attempt to answer skepticism: it fails because there are no "self-evident and convincing" first principles that can ground the rest. Hume's use of the word "convincing" is telling here. His point is not that there are no first principles—he is perfectly willing to grant, as we'll see later, that we must start somewhere. What he is suspicious of is the idea that we can defend those principles with reasons.

Hume's point here comes into bold relief when we consider his own most famous skeptical argument, which concerns whether we have reasons for believing things based on experience. As Hume correctly emphasized, this is how we come to believe most of what we come to believe. For example: I believe that eating bread will nourish me because it has done so before. Hume pointed out that trusting inferences of this sort (what philosophers call "inductive inference") seems as fundamental a principle as there is. After all, you can't give a mathematical (logical) *proof* that the baguette you ate today will be nourishing when you finish it tomorrow. Logical proofs require certainty, but we only get probability from experience. Nor can anyone "see" the future. So how can you show, asked Hume, that experience is a reliable guide to what will happen in the future? The only answer seems to be that you've learned it from experience: I think that my experiences in the past help me know what will happen in the future because they've done so in the past. But that's just to say that experience tells us that experience is reliable! We are back to where we've started. And this suggests that we can no more give reasons for our trust in making inferences from past experience than we can for our trust in observation.

Pause to appreciate how radical this is. The point isn't just that experience never gives us certainty. That is hardly news. Stuff happens; the world can change on us. The radical bit is that Hume is suggesting that we don't even have any reason to believe it is *probable* that bread will nourish us, that our brakes will stop our car, that the sun will rise tomorrow. We have no reason for it because we possess no noncircular reason to believe in the principle of induction.

*What Hume sees is that the problem Sextus raised was not about knowledge per se.*[10] What the skeptic wants is reasons, and not all knowledge comes with reasons. Much of what we know, we know the same way *animals* know.[11] Animal knowledge is the sort of knowledge we obtain just in virtue of being built a certain way, with certain natural abilities to process and intake information. Descartes also had this idea—he called it *cognitio*.[12] We acquire such knowledge from abilities as basic as vision, hearing, and taste—ways of accessing the world which work without us (or most of us, anyway) being able to explain *how* they work, let alone being able to defend their veracity against the skeptic. My three-year-old daughter can know that the cat is outside by looking. But she can't defend her views with reason. She just sees the cat. The skeptic says we don't know because we can't prove that our methods for gaining knowledge reliably produce true results. But the fact that my daughter can't *prove* that her method for knowing the location of the cat is reliable doesn't mean it isn't. Proving a point and knowing that it is true needn't amount to the same thing. Like other animals, humans can know without reflection—without knowing that they know.

But knowledge in this sense was never the real worry for Sextus. And it arguably wasn't the main worry for Descartes. Descartes was not just interested in *cognitio*—unreflective, animal knowledge; he was also interested in *scientia*—beliefs that can be defended publically by objective reasons.[13] This is hardly surprising. Reasons matter whenever it is up in the air whose methods you should trust, when there is open disagreement not only about what is known but about how to figure out what is known. And that was the position that Descartes found himself in. Proofs of the *possibility* of knowledge are fine and good. But what matters is whether we can *give* reasons—either to ourselves on reflection, or to someone who sees things differently. *That's* the problem that concerned Sextus, and which the Reformation reintroduced in sixteenth-century Europe. That's also the problem, as we saw in chapter 1, that some contemporary critics of science are keen to raise. It is a problem, as Hume knew, Descartes never solved. The real question is whether Hume is right that no one can.

## 3  Skepticism and Epistemic Incommensurability

Skepticism about reason is not just an abstract philosopher's thought experiment. It can arise whenever we get into deep and abiding disagreements about epistemic principles—principles which tell us what is rational to believe because they tell us what sources of belief we should trust.

In most cases where we question each other's principles—as might happen when one doctor questions another about the reliability of a given test—the dispute is settled by an appeal to other, more basic principles. We can put this by saying that most disagreements over epistemic principles are relatively shallow. They can be resolved, at least hypothetically, given enough time and so on, by appeal to shared principles. What we might call "deep" epistemic disagreements, on the other hand, concern *fundamental* epistemic principles (or would so concern them were the basis of the dispute made explicit).

What makes a principle fundamental is that you can't justify it without employing the method that it endorses as reliable. For this reason, explicit defenses of such principles will always be subject to a charge of circularity.[14] Hume showed that the principle of induction is like this: you can't show that induction is reliable without employing induction. It also seems true of observation or sense perception. It seems difficult, to say the least, to prove that any of the senses are reliable without at some point employing one of the senses.[15] Similarly with the basic principles of deductive logic: I can't prove basic logical principles without relying on them.[16] In each case, I seem to have hit rock bottom: I can't argue for a basic epistemic principle without presupposing my commitment to it.

Induction and deduction are plausibly fundamental to everyone's worldview. They are absolutely fundamental. But not every principle that is fundamental to my worldview need be fundamental to yours. Moreover, some principles that are fundamental to my system will be *comparative*. They give weight, or trumping power, to certain principles over others. Most real epistemic disagreements are over these sorts of principles; they are over the scope of reason, over where to set its limits.

Here's an example. Imagine I get into a discussion about the origin of the planet with a "young-earth" creationist.[17] Creationists of this sort believe that God created the earth in six days, less than 10,000 years ago. Let's imagine a particularly consistent such creationist—call him Smith—who is familiar with the methods of science. Let's stipulate that he is sincerely interested in knowing what is true—as opposed to scoring political points. Smith does not claim that reading the Bible is the best way to know everything (like dentistry, mathematics or how to fix your car). He accepts that other methods for learning about the past (such as consulting the physical record) can be helpful; but he thinks that the Bible is the *most* reliable method for learning about the origins of the planet. In other words, the Bible trumps scientific methods in certain areas. When the physical or historical records and the Bible disagree with regard to something like the origin of the earth, Smith sides with the Bible. For him, this is a fundamental epistemic principle; it needn't be, perhaps, but let's imagine that it is. Asked to defend his decision, for example, Smith might say that the best he can do is to say that God inspired the Bible, that everything written in it is therefore true, and thus that it is the most reliable guide to the distant past. Asked how he knows this, Smith notes that the Bible says that God inspired it—in the past. And that, as Smith may well know, means that his reasoning is circular. But Smith has also read his Hume, and he points out that I am in a similar position. I think the best way to learn about the past is by developing the best explanation of the physical record. That's my fundamental principle. The simplest, most comprehensive hypothesis wins. But asked to defend this method, I must admit that it seems hard to do anything other than appeal to its track record of working—*in the past*. How do we know it worked in the past? What can I say? That's the simplest explanation of the data, of course!

Certainly, both of us might try defending our respective principles by an appeal to independent factors. The problem is that any such argument could itself easily turn out to be circular or push our disagreement back to the applicability of a different, equally contested method. This isn't always going to be the case; in fact, it mostly isn't. But here the issue is which method is best for learning about the *distant past*. Unless time-travel is an option, we can't check to see whether either method has produced accurate results by direct observation—and even if we could, that observation itself could be challenged.[18]

Don't get hung up on the toy example. Most young-earth creationists, unlike our clever friend Smith, don't know much science and are easy to catch on inconsistencies. The point is that our example still illustrates a deep worry, the very worry that (as Hume thought) doomed Descartes's project from the start. That worry is that deep down there is just no way to rationally resolve some debates over fundamental epistemic principles, for the simple reason that we can't rationally answer challenges to those principles.

To answer your challenges rationally, I must give you reasons. And not just any old reasons but reasons such that, were you to be aware of your principles and reason consistently with them, you would recognize them *as reasons*. They should be reasons that you can appreciate, in short. This is the notion of reason-giving that is in play whenever there is a need for coming to some mutually recognized agreement on some matter or course of action. Suppose we are wondering which of two plans for building a bridge is the safest, and we consult an engineer to find out. In so doing, we not only expect the engineer to be able to determine which plan is safer, but to be able to articulate (or otherwise make clear) the rational basis of her discrimination. In short, we expect her to give us a reason for favoring one plan over the other, a reason that *we can understand from our own standpoint*. Barring that, we will either not build the bridge at all or perhaps judge the plans to be equally safe and choose between them in some other way.

This constraint on reason-giving is consistent with some familiar distinctions. One might be justified in believing P without *having* a reason for that belief. The belief may simply be produced by a reliable method. Likewise one's belief might be *justified by a reason* without you *recognizing that it is a reason*. Moreover, one can have reasons one doesn't give or receive. But that is not what is at issue in the case of the engineer, or in the case of an overt epistemic disagreement. In both cases, there is a standing demand to *defend* our commitment to a particular principle by giving a reason that can be appreciated by what Hume called our *common point of view*. And to *epistemically* defend that epistemic principle requires giving some evidence to believe it that can be appreciated from our common point of view.[19]

This is the heart of the problem that Sextus raised and Montaigne and Hume later championed. Here, in brief, is the skeptical argument against the value of reason: You can defend a fundamental epistemic principle under challenge only if you can give a reason for that principle. Fundamental epistemic principles can be shown to be true only via circular arguments. Circular arguments can't be used to give reasons for believing anything. If I don't trust your methods, and therefore accept your principles, your reassuring me that they are reliable because employing them tells you so won't impress me. Nor should it.

The apparent upshot of this argument is that fundamental epistemic principles cannot be defended by appeal to reasons appreciable from a common point of view. Reason, as we might put it, can't defend itself. This point appears to have at least two alarming implications. The first is that disagreements over fundamental epistemic principles cannot be rationally resolved. For to rationally resolve a debate is to resolve it by appeal to reasons. But that would require, in this case, that fundamental epistemic principles be capable of being defended by reasons that can be appreciated from a common point of view, and the skeptical argument appears to show they cannot be defended by such reasons. To lift a term from Thomas Kuhn, it appears that our fundamental epistemic commitments can be *incommensurable* as far as reason is concerned.[20] And that, of course, is fuel to the skeptic's fire. For if I can't defend my most basic epistemic principles with reason, then what can I defend with reason?

If we forget the distinction between skepticism about knowledge and skepticism about reason made above, it might seem easy to resolve such disagreements. The winner is just the person who knows—in the animal, unreflective sense—that their principles are true.[21] But as we've already seen, this response is of little use in *resolving disagreement*. It is a platitude that a debate can be resolved only if there is some equally recognizable common ground between the participants. We may well know (via an epistemically circular argument, perhaps) which basic sources are reliable, and hence which epistemic principles are true. But that fact has absolutely no traction when one is trying to justify one's employment of a source in the face of open and explicit doubts about its reliability or the extent of its reliability. When posing a challenge to someone else's principles, it doesn't help to be told, "If you just accept the right principles then you'll be able to know that they're right." That answer offers stone instead of bread.[22]

The issue here, I hasten to emphasize, is not the pragmatic or political question of how best *in fact* to persuade others to "accept" our epistemic principles.[23] A big stick or a bribe is probably the most expedient method. Our question isn't about expediency but rationality. It is about whether it is even *possible* for reasons to move us when it comes to our fundamental epistemic commitments. As Descartes knew, the issue is at root an existential problem. It was not for nothing that he began his most famous work by talking about how he had come to change his mind about his most fundamental principles.

This brings us to the second alarming consequence of the skeptical argument. The skeptical argument seems to imply that we cannot understand how changing our minds about fundamental epistemic principles can be rational.

Imagine that Descartes comes to accept a fundamental principle on Tuesday that he did not accept Monday. He adopts a new fundamental principle that wasn't part of his previous repertoire. If he is to now recognize this change as having been rational, then he must be able to give a reason for this change that he knows his previous self would have recognized. He must think it possible to explain his later self to his earlier self. If he admits that he cannot do this, then it is mysterious how he could presently understand his change in view as one that was based on rational grounds. He may hold his new fundamental principle for reasons, but he cannot, on Tuesday, understand his *adoption* of it as being based on reasons. From this point, the argument takes a now-familiar form: any reason he could now give to his earlier self would be circular; and circular reasons wouldn't be accepted by his earlier self as reasons. If this is so, then the skeptic will say that it is hard to see how Descartes could see *his own change of mind* as having been rational.

This conclusion is mitigated slightly—but only slightly—by the fact that it leaves open the possibility that a negative change in epistemic view—transitions from holding a principle to not holding it—might well be recognizable as rational. But this is small consolation. For surely it is possible to improve one's epistemic situation by adopting new and more reliable sources of belief—including new basic sources. To do that is to commit to new fundamental epistemic principles, to improve your epistemic point of view. And it is obvious that such improvement is, or at least can be, a rational process—one based on reasons. And yet that is precisely what the above line of argument rules out. Epistemic incommensurability begins at home.

Which sources and principles we trust obviously matters. What we do depends on what we think it is rational to believe. What we think is rational to believe depends on our epistemic principles. And that means that what we do depends as much on our epistemic commitments as it does on our moral commitments. Skepticism about reason raises the possibility that we cannot give any public reasons for the epistemic principles we've committed to. Unless we can find some way to answer such skepticism, then the dream of putting our trust in the common principles of reason—the dream at the very core of the Enlightenment—will turn out to be nothing more than that, nothing more than dreams and smoke.

# 4  Reasons End: Tradition and Common Sense

## 1  That Is Just How Things Are Done

Reasons give out. From this the ancient skeptics concluded that we should stop believing. We moderns and postmoderns have been more sanguine. We are more inclined, with Wittgenstein, to shrug it off, to accept that "this game is played" and just keep on trucking. This appeals to our sense of ourselves as practical and realistic, and suggests that the right "answer" to skepticism is just to acknowledge the groundlessness of our believing, roll up our sleeves, and go on from there.

But go where exactly? If justification does come to an end, what fills the void? One answer goes like this: the central lesson is that when justification comes to an end, *tradition* takes over. All belief is framed by tradition—by historic, meaning-laden practices embedded within the fabric of one's culture.

Whether this is a good idea depends on what it means. Taken one way, the invocation of tradition reminds us that we are social animals, and how we think often depends on how we act. But taken another way, it encourages the disturbing and deeply illiberal thought that our traditional practices are beyond external criticism.

The first thing someone might mean by saying something like "all belief is framed by tradition" is that people inevitably reason in traditional ways. What reasons we give, and which reasons we recognize, depend on various traditions and customs. This is hard to deny. There a number of different ways that traditions serve to filter which reasons we recognize.

First, minds are creatures of habit. We think in patterns—even when those patterns can get us into trouble. People talk or text on cell phones while driving and defend it by saying that they've "never had an accident." This is of course terrible reasoning—but it is also incredibly common. Engaging in a risky behavior more than once doesn't make it less risky, but we think this way all the time.

Other patterns of reasoning are not so bad, of course. Expertise of any sort is built up out of long and wide-ranging experience with the subject or practice in question. That expertise informs the expert's opinions obviously, but it also informs how she reaches those opinions. Experts can often reach conclusions very quickly, just by "sizing up the situation." A good cook just knows what spices to add, and a chess master just knows how to get his opponent in check with the pieces on the board. Intuition like this is often due, as we noted in chapter 1, to ingrained patterns of reasoning—patterns that have been developed, particularly in the case of cooking and chess, by years of trying and developing techniques. And of course, the development of technique is itself generally due to traditional ways of teaching and learning chess and cooking skills. Just *how* traditional these techniques happen to be is often only apparent when someone breaks a tradition and does something unexpected. Often it is only in the face of innovation that people, including the experts, realize that they have been thinking within the confines of a tradition.

Thomas Kuhn famously argued that this same point holds for scientific practice. Scientific practice is infused with tradition as much as any other practice. Kuhn's way of putting this was that scientific investigation generally or "normally" proceeded within a *paradigm*. Paradigms "provide scientists not only with a map but also with some of the directions essential for mapmaking. In learning a paradigm, the scientist acquires theory, methods, and standards together, usually in inextricable mixture."[1] The "normal" scientist works on the problems recognized by the paradigm, but does not question the paradigm itself. Scientific revolutions occur when the paradigms themselves are challenged. Indeed, it is only then that they are recognized *as* paradigms or traditions, and not simply as "accepted fact." This is not too surprising once you think about it. New scientists are trained by scientists who were in turn trained by other scientists. Working scientists are handed down problems and sets of solutions, and educated in how to approach a problem—how to set up an experiment, how to evaluate it, how to communicate its results. What is handed down, in short, is a traditional way of doing things. As thinkers like Polyani have emphasized, this is often very good for the acquisition of knowledge. For while some of these traditions can be misleading and based on bad assumptions, many encode time-proven techniques and sound forms of reasoning (just as in cooking or chess).

So the idea that we form beliefs in traditional ways, that in some sense we must do so, whether we know it or not, seems right. In the writings of those who trumpet tradition, however, this sensible point is often conjoined with another.

Here, for example, is philosopher and social critic Alasdair
MacIntyre:

[It] is an illusion to suppose that there is some neutral standing ground,
some locus for rationality as such, which can afford rational resources
sufficient for enquiry independent of all traditions. Those who have
maintained otherwise either have covertly been adopting the standpoint of a tradition and deceiving themselves . . . or have simply been
in error. The person outside all traditions lacks sufficient rational
resources for enquiry and *a fortiori* for enquiry into what tradition is to
be rationally preferred.[2]

Read one way, MacIntyre is only reiterating the reasonable
points we just discussed: as a matter of fact, people reason in
set patterns, and it is naïve to think that they can "step outside"
of such patterns and make judgments that are free of them. Like
it or not, we are all born into at least some traditions, including
the traditions and practices that lace the very languages we grow
up speaking. Read another way, however, MacIntyre seems to
be suggesting that no judgment is *rational* independent of a
tradition. That is a very different thought, and one that has had
a role to play in the intellectual Left and Right.

Compare, for example, the conservative political thinker,
Michael Oakeshott:

Just as [a] scientific hypothesis cannot appear and is impossible to
operate, except within an already existing tradition of scientific investigation, so a scheme of ends for political activity appears within, and
can be evaluated only when it is related to, an already existing tradition
of how to attend to our arrangements.[3]

This passage is representative of a certain slide that can occur
when talking about knowledge and tradition. Notice that
Oakeshott *begins* with a statement of the plausible hypothesis
that any belief we form will always emerge against a background

of inherited assumptions and traditional ways of thought. Science also frames its hypotheses "within" paradigms. But notice how the passage ends: Oakeshott concludes not only that political reasoning always occurs within a tradition, but that it can be *evaluated only relative* to that tradition. That's the slide: we go from the true but innocuous claim that we reason traditionally to the more dubious but more exciting claim that tradition is that which sits at the end of any chain of reasoning.

Conservative intellectuals have trumpeted the importance of tradition for centuries on both sides of the Atlantic, starting with Hume's contemporary and the patron saint of many political conservatives, Edmund Burke, continuing right through Russell Kirk in the twentieth century. But Oakeshott insisted that the sins of liberalism weren't just political: they were epistemological. They involved, or so he thought, misconceptions about the nature of human knowledge.[4] The most central of these was liberalism's failure to appreciate that all beliefs are embedded within traditions, practices woven into a community, and to accept the severe limits of reason in politics.

The obvious question to ask the conservative traditionalist is, How do you know which traditions to follow? Traditions come in all flavors; some are good, others, well, not so much (such as the tradition in some cultures of killing women who have been raped, or the tradition of discrimination against black people by many white Americans). If all justification, all reasons, come to an end with tradition, it is not at all clear that we can answer this question. If all we can say (with Wittgenstein) is that "this game is played," but not also "this game isn't *worth playing*," then we seem to be in deep trouble.

Of course, many conservatives would like to think that while the skeptical arguments of Sextus and Hume show that reason can't ground itself, some other method of belief—say, religious faith—can do so. Reason can't get us to truth, but faith can. As saw in chapter 3, however, it is hard to see how this appeal to faith helps. The question immediately becomes: whose faith? "Well, *my* faith, naturally." The obvious problem is that if you punt this quickly on the practice of giving and asking for reasons for your views—if, to switch sports clichés, you throw in the towel and say that it all comes down to faith—you've left yourself with no way to rationally resolve disagreements over whose worldview is better. Indeed, you can't seem to say that any worldview is any better than any other.

All this is deliciously ironic. Conservatives love to decry what they perceive as liberalism's worship of relativism. Yet one of the core tenets of their view threatens to collapse into a remarkably similar position. Compare again the work of Thomas Kuhn, whose early work is also representative of the slide we saw in Oakeshott. It moves from an appreciation of tradition's inevitable role in shaping our thought to the view that nothing can be rational except relative to a tradition. Scientific change, he argued, should not be seen as the result of scientists coming to better appreciate reality. Rather he described it as more like a "conversion experience."[5] Scientific reasons only make sense in relation to a paradigm. Consequently, "proponents of different paradigms practice their trades in different worlds."[6] So, different scientific traditions are incommensurable:

[T]hey will inevitably talk through each other when debating the relative merits of their respective paradigms. In the partially circular arguments that result, each paradigm will be shown to satisfy more or less the criteria that it dictates for itself and to fall short of a few of those dictated by its opponent.[7]

There are no "external standards" by which to judge which paradigm is correct, and so we must give up on the idea that changing our scientific tradition gets us closer to the truth.

This is now a pretty familiar thought, and similar ideas have been defended by a number of prominent intellectuals, from Gadamer to Rorty. One difference is that progressives, like Rorty, tend to be more honest about its implications. Thus Rorty, who describes his view as a "cheerful ethnocentrism," remarks that

there is nothing to my use of the term "reason" that could not be replaced by "the way we Western liberals, the heirs of Socrates and the French Revolution conduct ourselves." I agree with MacIntyre and Michael Kelly that all reasoning, both in physics and ethics, is tradition-bound.[8]

Unlike conservative skeptics, Rorty is not claiming that a reliance on tradition will get us to the One True Story of the World. Tradition is not a better route to objective knowledge than reason. Nothing gets us to objective knowledge. In Rorty's view, inquiry is an evolving conversation. The key isn't to find some way to make everyone else shut up (by, for example, insisting that you and only you know the one Truth) but to find a way to keep the conversation going, despite our differences.

This is a praiseworthy stance. But one wonders on what basis it is maintained. Indeed, the differences between progressives like Rorty and conservatives like Oakeshott, while real and important in themselves, don't remove the fact that both invocations of tradition raise the same worry. If "reason" is just another word for "accepted by the tradition in which I live," then how can I respond rationally when the fundamental principles of my traditional practices are challenged? It appears that I can only shrug and say that this is the way we do things around here. The worry is that we are putting tradition itself outside of rational examination—outside of the game of giving and asking for reasons.[9]

A particularly instructive example is an influential figure I've already mentioned in passing—Ludwig Wittgenstein. As we've seen, Wittgenstein declared that justification came to an end; but the end in question was not an ungrounded *belief*, dogmatic or otherwise, but "an ungrounded way of acting."[10] These ways of acting, Wittgenstein emphasized, were not so much explicitly learned (in the way we learn something from a book, say) as acquired by observation and engagement in social practices. We learn how to act by being embedded in traditional forms of life, and these traditional ways of acting are where my chain of reasons ends. And consequently, my ways of acting are themselves without reason: "If the true is what is grounded, then the ground is not true, nor yet false."[11] Paradoxically, Wittgenstein thought, this fact is what made certainty possible; in "certain circumstances, a man cannot make a mistake." But that is not because there are special propositions that are somehow self-evident or prove themselves, as Descartes seemed to think. It is because the very idea of making a mistake about certain propositions makes no sense, because the very idea of *believing* them makes no sense. Our doubts, he says, depend "upon the fact that some propositions are exempt from doubt, are as it were like hinges on which those turn."[12] For Wittgenstein, the hinges of our belief are neither reasonable nor unreasonable, neither believed nor disbelieved; they simply are, "like our life."[13]

Wittgenstein's idea that it is actions, forms of life—not mere beliefs—that ultimately matter is striking. But it still leaves us with the question of how best to rationally defend those forms of life. Wittgenstein's answer, at least at times, appears to be along the following lines:

Where two principles really do meet which cannot be reconciled with one another, then each man declares the other a fool and a heretic. . . . I said I would "combat" the other man—but wouldn't I give him *reasons*? Certainly, but how far do they go? At the end of reasons comes *persuasion*. (Think of what happens when missionaries convert natives.)[14]

In one sense Wittgenstein is right. When you run out of reasons, and the stakes are high, the big stick comes out. You can't just sit around and talk to the Nazis. And big sticks are a very effective way of "persuading" people; so are advertising campaigns. Indeed, as Wittgenstein notes, missionaries, historically, have had great success converting natives through a combination of force and manipulation. But that very metaphor suggests that there is also a much darker thought in the neighborhood here. This darker thought is that changing people's minds—or changing our own minds—if the change is radical enough, can *never* be a rational process. Manipulation, conversion, power is all there really is. And is that really how we wish to understand our relationship to our own fundamental epistemic commitments? Is power how we should decide disputes over whether we should trust divine revelation or the methods of science when writing our textbooks?

I don't think so. The idea that tradition trumps reason is antithetical to democratic politics. To engage in democratic politics is to see one's fellow citizens as rational, autonomous agents who are worthy of equal respect under the law. Part of what it is to be an autonomous agent is to be capable of making judgments about what is rational to believe. Judgments about what is rational to believe are made on the basis of reasons.

I obviously would not respect you as a fellow judger if I were to refuse to give you a reason for some claim against you, should you ask for one; and likewise the state would fail to respect you, were it to refuse to give a reason for some use of its political power. And crucially, the reasons in question here cannot be reasons in the sense that my holding a gun to your head is "a reason for you to do what I want." Political claims on you cannot be justified, in a democratic conception of politics, by simply wielding or threatening brute force—for again, the imposition of a claim is not a justification of why that claim ought to be imposed. Rather, I must try to persuade you that my view is rational. Only then do I treat you as an autonomous being, a being who is capable of judging what to believe. Otherwise, by denying you access to whatever evidence is available, I am preventing you from making the judgment yourself, or even, in effect, making it for you. In sum, to the degree that we cease giving reasons for our views to each other—to the degree that we allow our disagreements to be resolved, and our governmental decisions to be made, without adequate reasons—to that degree we have ceased to conceive of ourselves as equal participants in a democratic enterprise.

What this shows is that again, the skeptical argument isn't just an abstract problem. It is a practical problem with political implications. And it isn't at all clear that the "tradition tradition" has anything useful to say. If you and I disagree over whose epistemic principles are true, saying to each other, "Well, my tradition sanctions this principle," is not going to help. I am not apt to countenance your tradition as sanctioning anything, and vice versa. In some cases we may live and let live. And that's good. But in other cases, where we have to mutually decide on some course of action, citing differing traditions doesn't seem to help; nor should it.[15]

Traditionalists, conservative or liberal, will no doubt say that I am interpreting their views in a bad light. Maybe so. But if all they mean is that traditional ways of thinking often put blinders on us, forcing us to recognize something as a reason over other reasons, I've already conceded that this is so. It just isn't going to help with Sextus's problem, nor does it show that what tradition steers us toward is better than that from which it leads us away. Nor will it help to point out that, in real life, when tradition is cited as a reason for doing or believing something, what is often meant is something like "the way we've been doing things around here is effective and useful." To say *that* isn't to invoke the tradition *itself*—it is to invoke the usefulness and effectiveness of that way of doing things, which is a matter that can be assessed independently. The same point holds if one maintains that inconsistent traditions can't be rational or that traditions increase in rationality as they increase in coherence.[16] This again seems plausible, but to make this point is just to concede that there are first epistemic principles—principles of logic—whose rationality is independent of tradition. And yet that is exactly what anyone must deny who thinks that Sextus's skeptical argument proves that reason comes to an end at tradition. After all, the *whole point* was that nothing is independent of tradition, in that all reasons ultimately end at a traditional commitment. Our traditional commitments or ways of acting are where the buck is supposed to stop, on this view. And that is why the view is so beloved of conservatives: its entire point is that at some point we just have to stop questioning and accept that "this is how things are done around here."

## 2 Common Sense and Presuppositions

So, "tradition" alone can't be our answer to skepticism about reason. And yet there is clearly something right about the idea. After all, we don't need some highfalutin' skeptic to tell us that we can't prove everything. Every adult knows they always have to take something for granted. But that doesn't stop us from having opinions.

Indeed, even Hume, the arch-skeptic, agreed with this. Hume didn't think that his arguments would make people stop trusting the basic sources of belief such as experience or observation. Should someone be convinced by Hume's skeptical arguments that he had no reason to trust, for instance, experience, Hume said, "he would nevertheless continue in the same course of thinking. There is some other principle which determines him to form such a conclusion. This principle is Custom and Habit."[17]

"Custom" is Hume's answer to where we land when reasons end. But this answer doesn't wear its interpretation on its sleeve. One way of interpreting it is to read "custom" as "tradition." But there is another way to read Hume here, which takes his point to be far more plausible. Elsewhere, he compared our tendency to trust reason to our tendencies to feel love for those who benefit us and hate for those who harm us. *It is just how we are built*:

All these operations are a species of natural instincts, which no reasoning or process of the thought and understanding is able either to produce or to prevent.[18]

And that, Hume is saying, is all there is to it. Whether we can defend our trust in reason is largely beside the point. Nature won't allow us to give up certain methods of belief, regardless of whether they are reliable.

Oddly enough, a very similar point was made by Hume's most ardent and intelligent contemporary critic, Thomas Reid. Like Hume, Reid was a Scot, but unlike Hume, he thought that skepticism was clearly false. His reasoning for thinking so is very similar to the point I just made. In Reid's view, it is a first principle that any given basic source or method of belief—such as those I've been identifying with scientific practice—is reliable. In Reid's view, such principles are shown to be self-evident by what he called "common sense":

If there are certain principles, as I think there are, which the constitution of nature leads us to believe, and which we are under a necessity to take for granted in the common concerns of life, without being able to give a reason for them; these are what we call the principles of common sense.[19]

For both Reid and Hume, then, there are principles that we must take for granted, such as "Observation is a generally trustworthy way of finding out about your environment." The peculiar thing is that Reid took this point to be a *refutation* of Hume. Why? In Reid's view, the fact that we can't help but believe certain principles means that they are "self-evident," and therefore epistemically rational.

Reid is right, of course, to agree with Hume that we have a natural instinct to trust observation and logical inference. We are hardwired that way. And there is a perfectly plausible evolutionary explanation for why this might be. We need to be able to navigate around our environment if we are to survive, and to be able to predict, at least to some degree, how the future might be given what we've experienced in the past. But these facts don't solve the skeptical problem about reason that we've been grappling with.

First, the fact that I can't stop believing certain principles (e.g., the principle that observation is reliable) doesn't mean that these principles are true, nor that I am justified in believing them to be. The indispensability of a principle, as we might put it, isn't a direct *epistemic* reason for my belief in that principle. Direct epistemic reasons are reasons to believe that something is true; and this is just the sort of reason Hume says we lack for our first principles. Thus, although the indispensability of a principle does, in fact, make it reasonable to commit to that principle, it doesn't prove that the principle is true.

Second, even if Reid were right about this—even if, in other words, the indispensability of certain principles really *is* an epistemic reason for them—indispensability itself isn't a reason we can give in defense of those principles, as Reid himself suggests in the passage above. And that matters, because (as I argued in chapter 3) the real problem is whether we can *give* reasons for our first principles, regardless of whether we take them to be matters of common sense. After all, one man's common sense is another's absurdity. We don't always agree on first principles, and neither do we always agree on which principles we have to take for granted.[20]

Here's an example. There is an version of Christian apologetics known among its many advocates, online and off, as "presuppositionalism." According to this view, which was influentially formulated by Cornelius Van Til in the mid-twentieth century, core Christian beliefs are "presuppositions" of all rational thought. The very act of thinking rationally could not happen unless Christian beliefs were true. Hence, Christian beliefs cannot themselves be defended by reason, since by offering reasons we assume them already. You can't, in short, give reasons to believe in God that don't already assume—just because they are reasons—that God exists. And as a further, paradoxical result, it is no use arguing that God *doesn't* exist—because by doing so, one is already assuming that he does! As John Frame, one of the more erudite defenders of this position, admits, this has the look of circular reasoning: "God exists (presupposition) therefore God exists (conclusion)." But, says Frame, "this is unavoidable because God is the ultimate standard of meaning, truth and rationality."[21] A circle—but an unavoidable one.

Presuppositionalists acknowledge, of course, that not everyone sees the light. Other folks cling to other presuppositions, but in doing so, they ignore the one true presupposition. Indeed, because all thought presupposes Christianity in this way, non-Christians deny God not because they lack good reason, but because they are "rebellious." Frame quotes Paul's letter to the Romans in this regard:

What may be known about God is plain to them, because God has made it plain to them. For since the creation of the world, God's invisible qualities—his eternal and divine nature—have been clearly seen, being understood from what has been made, so that men are without excuse.[22]

Or as one charming zealot puts it on his website: "According to Scripture, all non-Christians are morons."[23]

Takes one to know one, I suppose. But the point I am making here isn't about Christianity per se, or even about presuppositionalist apologetics. My concern here is with the limits of Reid's point about common sense. Once you say that there are some principles which are self-evidently true because we all have to take them for granted—even though we can't give noncircular reasons for them—then how do you resolve the question of which principles those are?

Of course, just saying that your view is a presupposition of all thought doesn't make it so. It seems much more likely that logic is a presupposition in this way, for example, than any particular religious belief—if only because one can think and argue about many things—from cooking to chemistry—without ever relying on a particular religious view. And this means that *even if* "God exists" is a presupposition, and therefore immune to reason, it doesn't follow that "The belief that God exists is a presupposition" is so immune. In other words, presupposition-alists still have to give an argument for why we should think that their beliefs *are* presuppositions—and presumably they must give this argument even if, as I said, they really are presuppositions. Of course, any such argument will have to presume the rationality of the core beliefs in question. If you aren't convinced that God exists then you won't be convinced that you can't rationally deny God's existence. Hence, it is not clear what sort of argument a presuppositionalist could give for their view that their beliefs are presuppositions which wouldn't end up with the dogmatic assertion that it just is a presupposition that their beliefs are presuppositions.

The same issue arises with Reid's commonsense strategy. If you say that it is self-evident that S is reliable *because* we all must take it for granted that S is reliable, then what do you do if someone challenges you on this "fact"? Presumably, you inform them that they are relying on S's reliability when they challenge you. And maybe they are. Indeed, *if* they are, then they're actively engaged in undermining their own position. But nothing has been said, so far, to prove the principle that S is reliable to someone who doubts both the principle and your claim that it is a fundamental presupposition. The "common-sense" strategy still leaves those questions open.

Once you open the door to the thought that certain principles are true but need no defense by reason, you face being charged with dogmatism. As I'm using the term, the dogmatist holds his position and refuses to support it in the face of public challenge. Dogmatism of this sort might not be a big deal if our only worry were whether we *know* that our epistemic principles are true. But as I argued in chapter 3, it isn't. The skeptics can happily admit that we can know, in the *animal* sense, without being able to give reasons to anyone, including ourselves, for thinking as we do. The problem is not knowledge per se. The problem is *whether we can show that we have such knowledge by giving public reasons—reasons that can be appreciated from a common point of view.*[24]

The third and final problem with Hume's and Reid's indispensability argument is that it only deals with the easy cases. The easy cases, so to speak, concern fundamental principles like "Observation is generally reliable." But when religious people question whether science is as reliable as religious authority in discerning the truth of some matter, they aren't generally suggesting that we should throw science out entirely. This, in part, was the point of my discussion of young-earth creationists in the last chapter. *Real* doubts about reason are generally doubts about its *limits*. That is hardly surprising. Giving up on reason entirely, as both Hume and Reid emphasized, would be self-defeating: we have to trust observation, logic, and so on, to *some extent*, whether we like it or not. So the hard question isn't: Is observation worth trusting, period? The hard questions concern whether we should trust observation more or less than other sources of belief in specific contexts. In short, the hard cases concern what I have called *comparative* fundamental principles.

So appealing to our natural instincts isn't going to get us out of this problem; but it is nevertheless a step in the right direction. There are certain sources of belief, and therefore certain principles, we must take for granted without being able to give epistemic reasons for them. But this doesn't mean that we can't provide reasons for what we take for granted. It just means that the reasons we can provide must be of a different kind.

# 5 The "Sacred Tradition of Humanity"

## 1 Belief, Faith, and Commitment

The nineteenth-century British mathematician and philosopher W. K. Clifford is often portrayed as a poster-boy for reason. That doesn't really do the man justice; but it is true in its way. Before his death at the age of thirty-four, Clifford anticipated aspects of Einstein's theory of relativity, invented an algebra later named for him, married the novelist Lucy Clifford, wrote a book of children's stories, and even survived a shipwreck off the Italian coast.[1] But today he is mostly remembered, if at all, for a single essay, "The Ethics of Belief," an impassioned, if rather severe, defense of the importance of reason. This 1877 essay still has lessons to teach us, and I'll use it as a jumping-off point for my own positive defense of the value of reason.[2]

Clifford's stance is uncompromising: "It is wrong always, everywhere, and for any one, to believe anything upon insufficient evidence." He first introduces this point with a story about a ship. Here's the reality TV version: Not long ago, a major American airline was fined millions of dollars by the FAA for neglecting to perform fatigue-crack inspections on its Boeing 737s. Such reports raise some obvious questions: Did the executives involved willingly ignore the inspections, or did they simply convince themselves, perhaps over time (and without even knowing it) that these costly inspections were unnecessary? Either way, as the song says, "Somebody did somebody wrong." For even if the airline's executives sincerely believed that the airplanes were safe, they should have done the inspections anyway. After all, the point of the inspection is to *determine* whether an airplane is safe; safety is not something you guess about. And here we have Clifford's point: Even if the executives did believe their airplanes were safe, and even if, luckily, they really were safe, these executives had no right to believe so without any evidence.

In short, Clifford's argument for thinking it is always wrong to believe on insufficient evidence is that beliefs are tied to action. We decide what to do (fly) because of what we believe (the airplane is safe). So, since belief is tied to action, believing *without* sufficient evidence (as did the executives, above) can lead to actions that hurt or kill other people. And that's wrong.

This, of course, is an entirely sensible point. Yet ever since it was written, Clifford's essay has been a lightning rod for criticism. Most of this criticism, not surprisingly, has come from those who wish to defend the rationality of religious belief. The conservative writer David Berlinski, for example, seethes that Clifford's view "functions as a premise in a popular argument for the inexistence of God . . . if there is insufficient evidence for the existence of God, then it must be wrong to believe in his existence."[3] Clifford is regarded by Berlinski as the standard-bearer for the lab-coated thugs of the mainstream scientific community. In Berlinski's eyes, Clifford, and anyone who agrees with him, is condemning religion.

Curiously, Berlinski fails to notice that Clifford's "popular" argument for the "inexistence of God" is actually no such thing. After all, the conclusion of Clifford's *actual* argument, summarized just above, is not that God doesn't exist, but that it is wrong to believe anything on insufficient evidence. So even if we were to assume, for the sake of argument, that there is insufficient evidence for the belief that God exists, it would only follow, according to Clifford, that we would be wrong in believing he exists. It doesn't follow that we should believe he doesn't. Berlinski isn't the only one to overlook this point. No less than the great psychologist and philosopher William James fell into the same confusion in writing his response to "the *enfant terrible*" Clifford. According to James, it is permissible to believe in God without sufficient evidence because religious belief is an example of a forced decision: you have to either believe in God or not. But that is a mistake: not believing that God exists isn't the same as believing that God doesn't exist. I may not believe that "the butler did it," but that doesn't mean that I think he is innocent either. The jury may still be out, as we say. Similarly, Berlinski and James imply, wrongly, that there are only two options here: believing that God exists or believing that he does not exist. But in fact, there is a third option: *being undecided*. Clifford's point is simply that if the evidence doesn't swing you one way or the other, then you have no business believing one way or the other.

Nonetheless, Clifford's argument clearly oversteps the mark. We can all agree with him that doing what the airline executives did is wrong: not acquiring sufficient evidence can get people hurt. But it doesn't follow that it is *always* wrong to believe on insufficient evidence. After all, the skeptical argument shows that we can't give evidence for everything, even if we want to.

When it comes to our most fundamental epistemic principles, giving evidence for them is impossible without circularity. Nonetheless, we'll believe them anyway. We have to take something for granted. As Hume says, this is just the way we are built. My "natural instincts" make me trust certain methods of belief whether I can give evidence for their reliability or not. I can't be blamed for this.

This looks like a victory for faith, and in a sense it is. But only in a sense. It shows that Clifford's negative argument—his criticism of unbased belief—oversteps. But Clifford also has another point to make, a point that is often overlooked:

> The danger to society is not merely that it should believe wrong things, though that is great enough; but that it should become credulous, and lose the habit of testing things and inquiring into them; for then it must sink back into savagery.[4]

This "habit" of testing and inquiring is, I think, what really concerned Clifford. The problem with shoddy methods is that they lead to shoddy beliefs, and that in turn leads to even shoddier methods and habits of inquiry, and so on. "The sacred tradition of humanity," Clifford writes, "consists, not in propositions or statements which are to be accepted and believed on the authority of tradition, but in questions rightly asked, in conceptions which enable us to ask further questions, and in methods of answering questions."[5] In short, Clifford isn't just scolding us. He is telling us that we should commit ourselves to a particular attitude of open inquiry, and the principles that follow from it. If it is a tradition, he suggests with more than a little irony, it is a tradition of not abiding simply by tradition—of thinking things through, insofar as we can, for ourselves.

Clifford is sometimes criticized for inappropriately assigning moral concepts like blame and responsibility to *believing*. This is inappropriate, the thought goes, because we can only be blamed (or praised) for what we can control. We don't directly control our beliefs: you either feel that something is true or you don't.[6] This point undercuts the letter of Clifford's view, but not the spirit. For while you may not be able to control your beliefs directly, you can control other things that affect what you believe. You can control how you go about conducting an inquiry, which questions you ask, what sources you consult, and which methods you use in handling your data.

More generally, we are responsible for our commitments, including our commitments to principles. To commit to a principle is to adopt the policy of relying on it as true, of using it as a premise in our deliberations over what to think or do.[7] Commitment is distinct from belief. It is different from belief because one can commit to a principle without believing, like the scientist who commits to a theory, and so relies on it in subsequent reasoning, while remaining agnostic about its ultimate truth. You can also believe without commitment—you can find yourself feeling that something is true without thinking it wise to adopt a policy of acting on that feeling. Commitment is also not mere assumption. To really commit to a principle means commitment to its truth, such that one no longer plans further inquiry into the matter. One takes the issue to be closed unless and until further considerations force you to reconsider.[8]

The real lesson to take home from Clifford, then, is not the command: Thou shall not believe without sufficient evidence. That is a law we cannot help but break. The real lesson is that it is crucial for the good of civil society to commit to the ideal of reason. Committing to this ideal has something in common with the pose of the skeptic. We should be willing, Clifford says, to ask questions, to look for explanations. But carried to its furthest extreme, as Sextus showed, the skeptic is someone who *only* questions—who never commits. And that is not a way to live a life. It is not just questions, but *questions rightly asked* that Clifford says are important. In short, the ideal of reason Clifford is trumpeting brings with it commitments to epistemic principles, principles that recommend methods, and practices which allow us to "ask further questions." This is the attitude of one who trusts in reason, and it is precisely a lack of it that Clifford thinks is damaging to our society.

In this book, I've been using the word "reason" to talk about the fundamental epistemic principles that are constitutive of scientific practice. Our paradigm examples have been principles that privilege controlled observation, induction, and logical inference. These principles tell us which sources of belief should be trusted. Hume and the skeptics are right that we have to trust those sources without evidence.[9] But reflection on Clifford's argument tells us what trusting reason—having faith in it—really amounts to. To have faith in reason is to commit to these fundamental epistemic principles—that is, to adopt a policy of using logical inference and observation in as unstinting and open-minded a way as possible. In so doing, I commit to these sources being reliable even though I cannot show that they are reliable without employing them. But this commitment, this faith, isn't *blind*. I can justify my fundamental principles. I can justify them by showing how important these principles are for a functioning civil society. I can give what philosophers call *practical reasons* for them. Practical reasons are reasons for doing something given our aims, projects, and conceptions of the good. They are the sorts of reasons we typically give in moral and political debates. Committing to a principle is an act—it amounts to adopting a policy of using that principle, and therefore of relying on the sources it recommends as reliable. So even if my epistemic reasons for my fundamental epistemic commitments run out, that doesn't mean I can't provide reasons for trusting one source over another, since I can still provide practical reasons for committing to those principles. That's the sort of argument I gave in chapter 4 against taking tradition as our stopping point. And it is the sort of reason that Clifford himself hints is possible in defending our commitments to principles at the heart of science.

This is the strategy I will develop in this chapter: I will give an argument for the practical rationality of reason. The sort of reasons I aim to uncover are reasons we can give, in the sense explained in chapter 2, to those who challenge our fundamental epistemic commitments, and which we could use to assess those commitments. They are, in short, public reasons. Now obviously we can't just start coming up with a list of specific reasons for each and every one of the epistemic commitments we might happen to have. That wouldn't be very helpful, even if it were possible. Rather, the strategy must be to find a procedure—a way of identifying good reasons to make an epistemic commitment. I spell out and defend just such a procedure in this chapter.

Prior to doing so, however, let me briefly lay out what sort of procedure I *won't* be following. Doing so will allow us to understand two important constraints that I believe any serious argument for the practical rationality of an epistemic commitment must meet.

We've already seen one sort of bad practical reason someone might give for an epistemic commitment. You might claim that a commitment is rational because the principle in question is endorsed by your tradition, is part of a socially entrenched form of life, or is otherwise adopted by those in the know.[10] We saw that this appeal was not very convincing; among other things, I argued that it was undemocratic.

A second strategy worth mentioning—and rejecting—is that we should commit to those epistemic principles that maximize our preferences. In other words: the rational epistemic commitments are those that make the greatest number of us the happiest. This might work if we all had the same preferences. But if we are already disagreeing over fundamental epistemic principles, we probably don't. After all, people want all different sorts of things. Some of them are noble, while many are, well, less so. And many of them conflict: We want small government, for instance, but we want a big military; we want to eat donuts but we want to be slim. And we want epistemic principles that help us get at the truth, but we also want "facts" that confirm what we already believe. So even if we were somehow able to take the average of all our preferences, or only took the value of some particular, widely shared subset of our preferences, we could still end up endorsing a contradictory set of principles, not to mention ones that end up simply telling us what we want to hear. Presumably no one, liberal or conservative, would think this is a very good idea. It seems to be the high road to epistemic disaster.

But doesn't this overlook the most obvious reason to commit to an epistemic principle? Consider scientific principles. One might think the most obvious reason to commit to such principles is that they get results. It is science that builds our bridges, heats our houses, and cures diseases. And that alone seems to make it extremely rational to commit to scientific principles. They are simply more useful than other epistemic principles.

I agree. Indeed, it is hard to see who wouldn't. Science is useful. But making this point isn't going to help us here, because focusing on science's achievements won't really answer the skeptics about reason. For one thing, skeptics about scientific reason are rarely if ever skeptical about it across the board. Their quarrel is with its use in certain domains. And further, whether you find science trustworthy because it gets results depends on whether those results are ones you want. Further still, the question of whether scientific reason gets us what we want more than other methods is partly what is at dispute, since science's success at getting us what we want hinges, presumably, on whether its methods are a reliable means to the truth. And that, of course, can be challenged. People who think that the Torah or Bible or Koran is a better means to the truth about the origin of our planet, for example, do just that.

So while the above sorts of reasons won't help us, reflecting on them is helpful. We are looking for a way of identifying reasons we can appeal to when our fundamental epistemic commitments are challenged. What our reflections suggest is that any good procedure for identifying reasons must meet two constraints. Each constraint asks us to abstract away from certain features of our situation.

First, we need a way of identifying reasons to commit to principles that abstracts from our actual preferences. Otherwise we'll just be giving "reasons" to favor principles from the standpoint of our own value systems and prejudices. Reasons like that are not objective in the required sense: they won't be recognized as reasons by anyone who doesn't already share our standpoint.

Second, we need a way of identifying reasons to commit to principles that abstracts away from their truth. The skeptical argument shows that we can't give epistemic reasons for our most fundamental epistemic principles; so if we are going to avoid begging the question, we need a way of picking out reasons that doesn't already suppose that certain epistemic principles are true.

My strategy for meeting these constraints unfolds in two parts. The first part argues that the fundamental epistemic principles constitutive of scientific practice have a distinctive "open" character. They generate "public" reasons—reasons that are assessable from a common point of view. The second part argues that it is practically rational to commit to those fundamental principles which have this virtue, regardless of skeptical objections, and indeed that we should privilege them relative to other fundamental principles.

## 2   Objectivity and a Common Point of View

Here is one way to put our question: What reasons could we give for trusting scientific methods and practices over others? As I noted above, rather than focusing on science's achievements, I'll focus on how it goes about accomplishing them. Scientific methods have virtues independently of their results.

In order to see how a practice or method can get something right, it sometimes helps to see how it can go wrong. Case in point. In 1998, Dr. Anthony Wakefield and several other researchers published an arresting article in the prestigious British medical journal, the *Lancet*. This article alleged that there was a causal relationship between the measles-mumps-rubella (MMR) vaccine and autism in children. The impact of the article was large. Following its publication, rates of inoculation fell alarmingly in the United States, Ireland, and Britain, and the incidence of measles outbreaks increased.[11] Moreover, the article served to fuel the fire of a general skepticism about inoculations and vaccines already existing in several countries.

The *Lancet* is an extremely important scientific publication. Getting an article accepted by its editors is no mean feat, and this one had passed the various tests. Nonetheless, the study was immediately subjected to criticism by researchers who were skeptical of its results and of the methods used to reach them— including the authors' small sample set of data. Subsequent attempts to duplicate the findings failed. In 2009, journalists helped discover that the data itself had been extensively tampered with; the findings were declared fraudulent; Wakefield was fired from his research position as a result, and the journal withdrew the article from circulation.

Cases like this are unsettling. They show that the "scientific establishment" is open not only to error (bad results can be published in good journals), but to corruption. Scientists eager for fame or money or simply wishing to verify results they think they already "know" can alter data, sometimes with disastrous results. Science, as an institution, is subject to the same errors and problems as any other institution; that scientists sometimes lie, or less darkly, simply do poor experiments, should come as no surprise. But it still does surprise, simply because we have become accustomed to scientists being portrayed as steely-eyed seekers of the truth. And some are. But as with any profession, scientists come in all types. Some are good, some are honest, while some are less so—and some are perhaps neither.

The Wakefield case also shows something else, however. People sometimes put it like this: science is a self-correcting enterprise. The errors in Wakefield's scientific work were first pointed out by other scientists; its initial skeptics were other scientists. When science goes wrong, doing more science can help to show us that it has gone wrong. This sets science apart from practices that are by nature insulated from correction. Consider the presuppositionalists we discussed in chapter 4, or some versions of psychoanalysis, according to which any denial of the theory is a confirmation of its accuracy. Theories that, in effect, insist they are always right are not self-correcting because, at least by their own lights, they aren't capable of any correction—which, of course, is precisely why we should not trust them. But there are still other methods besides science that can lay claim to being self-correcting. If what someone thinks is revealed by God is not in fact so revealed, then (it might be said) more divine revelation could correct this error. Of course, all this assumes that divine revelation is a reliable "method" of belief-formation in the first place, and that is questionable. But it points to a more general lesson: a method can't be self-correcting if it isn't capable of being correct in the first place. And more importantly for our purposes: a method we can't defend from challenge as correct we aren't going to be able to defend from challenge as self-correcting, either.

Nonetheless, the idea that science is self-correcting gets at something about the principles that underlie scientific methods that sets them apart from others. Scientific principles of inquiry have certain features that lend them a distinctively open character. That is, the reasons generated by such principles are public reasons—reasons that can be appreciated from the common point of view. I don't take it to be particularly controversial that science has these features, even for skeptics about reason. And that, as we'll see, is part of my point.

First, science, and the assessment of scientific results, is a group enterprise. The success of a scientific investigation, over the long term, is not judged by any one person or set of persons but by a larger public or group. Scientific judgments in this sense are *intersubjective*. Of course, the people who do the relevant judging in science are generally other specialists. But this set of specialists includes not just the experts of the moment, but experts across time. It is the long haul that matters for scientific assessment. That is, in order to receive any credibility whatever, a scientific study must be reviewed by peer scientists from the outset, including peers who put their stock in rival hypotheses and theories. And importantly, as the Wakefield episode discussed above indicates, this process of critical review does not end with the publication of the work in a reputable journal.[12] Testing and attempts to duplicate experiments can, and often do, continue after the work is published. Moreover, this work is continually open to public refutation by additional work in the future.

Scientific practice is also relatively *transparent*. Scientists' careers hinge on their success in publishing their work in peer-reviewed journals. But the point of these journals is not just to provide a stamp of approval. Journals, along with conferences and seminars, exist so that scientific work can be shared. This means that the various people working on scientific problems don't have to constantly start over, but can build on the work of others. But this sharing, and the relative transparency it involves, also opens the data to question and possible refutation—to public assessment, in other words. Indeed, the expectation of transparency in science is so strong that when violations occur—or even appear to occur—it can draw the media's attention and cause genuine outrage. The so-called Climategate scandal of a few years ago is an illustration. In 2009, hacked emails from British climate scientists were alleged to reveal two things: first, that scientists were deliberately "hiding" data that were (supposedly) inconsistent with global warming, and second, that they were preventing publication of articles incompatible with their own views. In 2010, an independent UK government inquiry (actually several) found that these charges were largely false. Critics of climate change predictably described this as a whitewash, just as members of the Texas Board of Education have alleged that scientists have rigged the data for evolutionary theory. Neither allegation is warranted, but the fact that such claims are even made supports my point here: Transparency is a well-entrenched and assumed scientific norm, appeal to which often plays a role in political discussions involving science. Transparency is part of the public character of science, and that is why people are so quick to run to the rooftops when they perceive a failure in this transparency.

The relative transparency and intersubjectivity of scientific principles and methods are part of what gives scientific practice what I earlier called openness—that allow it to produce reasons and evidence we can judge from a common point of view. But there are at least three other elements worth noting. First, scientific methods—and the more basic methods on which they in turn rely—are highly *repeatable*. By that, I mean that in like cases they give like results. The idea that a sound experimental methodology will allow for subsequent repetition and therefore possible confirmation (or disconfirmation) of results is, of course, familiar. But it is worth emphasizing that repeatability is a feature of the most basic methods and sources of belief that science draws upon. Consider, for example, perceptual observation. If I look and perceive a chair in the room, and then look again in the same conditions—that is, where the lighting, my vision, and so forth remain the same and no one enters or leaves the room—I will most likely perceive the chair again. The situation is similar with logical deduction. If I prove a theorem one day and can prove it again the next, the results—assuming I am inferring correctly—will be the same from one day to another.

Second, basic methods like observation, deduction, and induction come naturally to humans. They are, as Hume said, part of our natural instincts. They are the only methods that are uncontroversially hardwired into us. Most people can employ them at least to some degree. Third, these same basic methods are also extremely *adaptable*. Indeed, the very essence of logic is that it can be applied to any problem; and while perception is hardly that adaptable (we can't use it to solve abstract mathematical problems, for example), we can and do use perception to help us address a vast array of questions.

In sum, then, part of what makes scientific practice distinctive is that it is comparatively intersubjective, transparent, repeatable, natural, and adaptable. These features give science its open character, and the application of its methods can be judged relatively publicly and independently. Compare the methods of divine revelation or the practice of consulting the Bible to learn about the origin of the planet. Putting aside whether these methods are in fact reliable, it is clear that neither is as intersubjective or transparent as scientific methods. Their success (or failure) is a matter of private judgment, and their results are not open to pooling or sharing in the same way as experimental results. It is not surprising to anyone that disagreements among those who employ such methods aren't open to independent adjudication. Indeed, it is precisely this fact—that they obviously aren't open to public adjudication in the way that scientific methods are—that has caused advocates of religious doctrines like creationism or "intelligent design" to try so hard to make their views at least seem scientific. Doing so makes their views, and the methods they use to derive them, seem to be more objective—and thus, more worthy of being taught in public schools.

But the features that make scientific principles open don't just distinguish scientific practice from religious practice. Appealing to these virtues can also help us determine whether a given scientific practice is worth trusting (or is as trustworthy as other scientific methods). In 2010, Harvard psychologist Marc Hauser's research on language involving tamarin monkeys was found to be marred by tampered data.[13] But prior to this exposure, questions about his work were already extant, precisely because his methods resisted replication. Hauser claimed, for example, that his tamarin monkeys passed the Gallup test (self-recognition in a mirror), while the fact that this result resisted replication by other researchers was attributed, by Hauser's supporters, to his superior skill in interpreting the movements of tamarin monkeys and to the fact that there are so few primate labs. Whether or not this is correct (and it is difficult to see that it is, in light of the subsequent revelations of a Harvard investigation), appeals to the values of transparency and repeatability were at the heart of the various judgments of Hauser's work.

So the principles that underlie science are open in character because the methods they recommend can be used to generate public reasons. This in turn explains why we take such reasons to be objective. Objective reasons are reasons whose force does not hinge on any particular person's point of view. The features that give scientific principles their distinctive sense of openness also explain why we take the reasons generated by those principles to be objective, at least in one sense of that word.

Objective reasons are impartial—we can judge them as reasons from a shared, common point of view. But we must be careful; that doesn't mean they are free from all subjectivity.[14] Objective reasons are not "value free." That would be impossible, since epistemic principles, as I've understood them in this book, *are* values: they tell us what sources and methods of belief to trust. What matters for objective reasons is not whether they can be assessed from *no* point of view—from the "view from nowhere," so to speak—but whether they can be assessed from *many* points of view. Reasons are objective to the degree that their truth or falsity can be *judged from diverse perspectives*.[15] That is what is meant by a common point of view. Such reasons are those that we can assess without just having to take someone's word for it. We can, at least to some extent, go check for ourselves. Hence, when we talk about "objective reasons" it is not just truth or falsity that matters but rather *the manner in which that reason can be judged*. Objectivity in this sense is a matter of openness to evaluation from a common point of view.[16]

## 3   The Method Game

The overall plan I'm pursuing is this: just because we can't give epistemic reasons for our fundamental epistemic principles to those who doubt those principles, doesn't mean that we can't give reasons for those principles. More precisely, we can give reasons for being committed to our principles, where to be committed to a principle is to be willing to act on it, to employ the method it recommends as reliable. We can defend our epistemic commitments in the same way we can defend any commitment—by giving practical or ethical reasons. So far, we've noted that some principles—those that seem to underlie science—can be used to generate public reasons appreciable from a common point of view. You might think that this already shows that it is rational to commit to such principles. And in a way, it does—but only as long as you are *already willing to value open principles*.

What this means is that we are only halfway to our goal of defending the rationality of reason. We've shown that certain sorts of epistemic principles—including those at the heart of (ideal) scientific practice—generate objective, public reasons. What we now need is an argument that is itself based on public reasons for the practical rationality of committing to such principles. We need to show that the principles that allow us to have a common point of view are themselves justifiable from a common point of view.

I think we can give such an argument. Its core idea is that *the fundamental principles we should be committed to are those that persons concerned to advance their interests would endorse in a position of epistemic and social equality*. The principles that would be endorsed in such a position are open and objective. So it is rational to commit to such principles.

I'll develop this point by appeal to a thought experiment about an imaginary game. The object of this game is to decide, jointly with other players, the fundamental epistemic commitments of the inhabitants of a hypothetical planet I'll call "Parallel Earth." Fundamental epistemic commitments are commitments to fundamental epistemic principles. Such principles are epistemic because they tell us which sources and methods of belief to trust; they are fundamental because they recommend sources or methods that can't be shown to be reliable without employing those very sources or methods. A relatively uncontroversial (and by now very familiar) example would be:

LOGIC:   Deductive inference from true premises is a reliable method for forming beliefs.

Not all examples are like LOGIC, however. Some fundamental principles—particularly the controversial ones—take a comparative form, weighing the reliability of one method against another. For instance:

PAST:   The most reliable method for learning about the past is abduction from the historical and fossil records.

This is one of the principles under issue in the "imaginary" debate we had with a young-earth creationist in chapter 3, who claimed, on the contrary, that the best method for learning about the primeval past, and in particular, the origin of the planet, is to read the Bible.[17]

The players of this imaginary game, let's call it "the method game," will be asked to decide on which such principles should be privileged on Parallel Earth, where a principle is privileged when the method it recommends is widely employed and the principle itself is taught in the schools, used to decide between research proposals, and the like. In short, privileged principles are those to which Parallel Earthians are committed. The game is played in rounds. A pair of fundamental principles is laid on the table by a referee, and the players then rank the principles in accordance with the object and rules of the game. A principle wins the game just when it wins more rounds than it loses over all rounds played. In short, the game is a bit like *Survivor!* for epistemic principles.

In making their decisions in the method game, the players must always bear three important things in mind. Think of these as the rules of the game. First, players of the game will eventually have to join this society on Parallel Earth. They don't live there now, but they will. So the decisions they make now about which principles Parallel Earthians should adopt will end up making a difference in their lives and their children's lives. Second, players don't know what social position they will later occupy on Parallel Earth. By this, I mean that they don't know what their relative educational level, ethnicity, or social class will be on Parallel Earth. So, in making their decisions during the game they would be wise *not* to privilege epistemic principles that would only help the socially privileged on Parallel Earth. And third, and most important, players don't know *which principles will be true, which methods and sources of belief formation will actually be reliable* on Parallel Earth. They don't know *here* which methods are more likely to result in true beliefs *there*. Indeed, if you are playing the game, your level of ignorance about this is vast. As far as you would know, none of the methods anyone will end up using on Parallel Earth will be reliable. This means that the simplest way of deciding which principles to privilege—by picking those that recommend methods that reliably produce truths—is off the table. Reliability, at least in this sense, is not something we can appeal to.

Our "game," of course, isn't really a game at all. It is a thought experiment, modeled after a very famous one by the political philosopher John Rawls. Rawls's version of the experiment was intended to justify certain principles of justice. His point was that the right principles of justice (particularly those dealing with the distribution of wealth) would be those "that free and rational persons concerned to further their own interests, would accept in an initial position of equality."[18] Which principles of justice should we accept? Those we would embrace if put behind "a veil of ignorance" from which we had no knowledge of our subsequent social position. From that position, it would be in our rational self-interest to adopt fair principles that only privilege the few over the many when doing so would benefit all. As I see it, we can adopt a modified version of Rawls's masterful idea for our situation as well.[19] Which epistemic principles should we accept? Those we would accept behind a double veil of ignorance: from which we have not only no knowledge of our social position on Parallel Earth, but also no knowledge of which of our doxastic methods and sources will be the most reliable there. The methods that should "win" an epistemic disagreement, in other words, should be those that would win more rounds of the method game. Why? Because, as I'll now argue, it would be in our rational self-interest to pick certain methods over others.

Before I can make this case, I need to unpack the details of this game a bit more. We can assume, for purposes of discussion, that the other players in the game are like us in certain minimal respects. They are human beings, and moreover, they know that they will remain so on Parallel Earth. Moreover, we can assume that the players of the game are all minimally intellectually capable, and able to engage in practical reason, both here and on Parallel Earth. By "practical reason," I mean the ability to give reasons for one's actions, to think about one's own self-interest, to form a conception of the good, and to engage in critical reflection on one's life. Finally, we can assume that the players of the game are not deceitful (or have no reason to be) and are not morally corrupt in any way that would be relevant to the successful playing of the game. These assumptions, of course, are idealizations, but they have a point: they allow us to abstract away from distorting factors.

When playing the game, the double veil of ignorance severely limits the sorts of reasons players can give for favoring one principle over another. In particular, in deciding which principles to privilege on Parallel Earth, the rules of the game prevent the players from appealing to any direct or indirect *epistemic* reasons for a principle. By "direct epistemic reason," I mean a reason to the effect that such and such method is more reliable, better able to get us to the truth, and so on, in the actual world or (so we imagine) on Parallel Earth. Thus, I am not allowed to reason that just because the actual world is such that observation is reliable, we should privilege observation on Parallel Earth. By "indirect epistemic reason," I mean an argument like this: Because God exists everywhere, he exists on Parallel Earth; God says that we should adopt method M; so, we should privilege any principle that recommends M on Parallel Earth. Likewise, I can't appeal to the fact that natural laws make observation more reliable than, say, astrology. In short, if we are to stay behind the double veil of ignorance, we have to foreswear appealing to any reason for favoring certain principles over others that involves an appeal, no matter how indirect, to that principle's truth.

So far, then, I've said what the players of the game are not allowed to do when constructing their reasons for thinking that a specific principle should be privileged on Parallel Earth. They can't appeal to any epistemic reasons and, given that they are all self-interested, they can't appeal to what we might call reasons of social prejudice (by dint of the fact that they don't know what their social position will be on Parallel Earth). So what can they appeal to? This, of course, is precisely the question the thought experiment is intended to get us to consider.

First, what sort of facts do they know about Parallel Earth? They know that the inhabitants of Parallel Earth will be humans. They know that they will be capable of engaging in practical reason; and they know that Parallel Earth will appear to them, in broad strokes, just as the actual world appears to us. Thus even if they don't know, in playing the game, whether observation will be reliable on Parallel Earth, they know that it will appear to be as reliable there as it does here. Likewise for all other methods and sources.

The players of the game will be able to appeal to this common set of facts in order to make their decisions. And this makes it likely that they will decide to follow Hume's advice and recommend adopting first and foremost those principles that we cannot help but trust—whether or not they are reliable. That is, given that the inhabitants of Parallel Earth are humans, and Parallel Earth appears to them as the actual world appears to us, it seems sensible that Parallel Earth people will have to take certain principles for granted whether or not the methods these principles recommend are really trustworthy or reliable. Why this is, of course, may depend on further facts about the Parallel Earth world that the players have no knowledge of; but they know enough, presumably, to conclude that once on Parallel Earth, they will still find themselves employing memory, observation, deduction, and induction. In short, we can imagine that in the early rounds of the game, various principles will be quickly voted on, simply because everyone will agree that human beings won't be able to prevent themselves from relying on the methods and sources they recommend, whether here or on Parallel Earth. Committing to such principles is part of our natural instincts. Call principles that are privileged for such reasons the *base set*.[20]

Unfortunately, it is also pretty clear that the game won't end there. For it will presumably be controversial among players of the game whether certain principles—those about mystical perception, divine revelation, rational intuition, and so forth—are members of the base set. So it will be controversial whether they "must" be privileged on Parallel Earth. And further, the scope of each of the principles in the base set (collectively or individually) will be controversial. Indeed, the real-life examples of epistemic disagreements that we've examined are of just this type. Everyone can agree that observation is something we have to rely on when crossing the road, but not everyone will agree that we must presuppose it when dealing with other matters.

This brings us to the second main type of reason that players of the method game will have available. Call these *reasons of practical value*. These are reasons to commit to a principle because it is, to some significant degree, in our rational self-interest to do so.

Which fundamental commitments would be in our self-interest is, of course, also a matter of debate. But I think it is fairly clear that were we to play the method game, it would be in our self-interest to privilege those fundamental principles on Parallel Earth which—on balance, and to the greatest degree possible—recommend methods that have the virtues we discussed above. That is, we should privilege principles that recommend methods and practices that are *repeatable*, *adaptable*, *intersubjective*, and *transparent*. Again, think about the constraints of the game. We don't know our future social position on Parallel Earth, and so (as I put it earlier) it won't be in our interest to privilege epistemic principles that privilege the socially privileged. Open principles generate reasons that can be objectively assessed—that is, assessed from a common point of view. In part, this follows from the fact that they recommend methods that are intersubjective, methods that are most effectively employed within groups. In part, it is also because they favor transparent practices, ones that (to some degree) produce results that can be shared and disseminated widely and are presented as being subject to critique. As a consequence, I argued, their seeming effectiveness could, in principle, be judged publicly[21]—that is, it is not the case that only a king, a president, or a priest is authorized to judge these methods' effectiveness. And this remains the case even if a given method is not in fact reliable and the principle in question is false. As I noted above, whether or not a principle can be objectively assessed is independent of whether it is true. In short, even if it would be in your self-interest, in the actual world, to commit to certain principles that are less open in character, it would be rational to commit to principles that are more open on Parallel Earth, given the rules of the game. It would be in your self-interest to favor such methods on Parallel Earth because you don't know if you'll be so lucky on Parallel Earth.

Under the rules of the method game, then, it will be practically rational to privilege what I called "open" fundamental principles precisely because they are open—the methods they recommend can be used to generate objective, public reasons. Scientific principles are like this. So it will be rational to privilege the fundamental principles which underlie scientific reason.

Of course, there are other considerations at work as well. One thing we know is that we'll continue to have to make plans on Parallel Earth. These plans will vary in scope and significance, from deciding what to do with whatever resources we end up with there to planning how to acquire more such resources. To plan, we need to form beliefs, and in order to form beliefs, we need methods of belief-formation. Again, we'd like to have reliable methods of belief-formation, but we can't appeal to reliability in playing the game. What we can appeal to, however, is a feature like repeatability. As noted above, a method is repeatable to the degree that it produces like results in like cases. It would be in our interest to favor more repeatable methods over less repeatable ones because the more repeatable methods' results, given enough information, would be predictable, and predictability is a necessary condition for useful planning. (This feature is not sufficient for usefulness of course—what makes a useful plan depends on context—but you've got to have some predictable way of gathering information if you are going to rely on that information to make decisions about what to do.) Again, all things considered, we clearly want methods that are repeatable *and* reliable at producing true beliefs. But if reliability is off the table, it still seems that repeatability *has value* for the simple reason that it would be difficult to practically rely on a method that told us to believe P today, but told us to believe not-P the next—even though the situation is the same.

Likewise, adaptable methods are those that can be employed on distinct kinds of problems and which produce results given a variety of kinds of inputs. It would be in our interest to favor such methods because we don't know what sort of problems we'll face on Parallel Earth. Logic, naturally, is a prime example of an adaptable method. You can use logical reasoning, reliable or not, to draw conclusions from any sort of premises.

The virtues we've been discussing, those that constitute openness, are not the only virtues to which we might appeal in sorting principles and methods in terms of their practical value. But they have much to recommend them. They are epistemically neutral, but not arbitrary; they are applicable to comparative principles and simple principles alike. Many methods, and applications thereof, will not have all of these features. Some will have none. And again, one method may have certain virtues to a greater degree than other methods, or possess one or more virtues to a greater degree than it possesses other features. None-theless, it seems plausible that for any epistemic principles $x$ and $y$, $x$ has more practical value than $y$ when the method that $x$ recommends has more of the above virtues, on balance and to a greater degree. The greater a principle's practical value, the more practically rational we would be to commit to it.

We might have to balance the relative practical value of a fundamental principle against other factors. Some may argue, for example, that the inhabitants of Parallel Earth cannot help but use what mathematicians have sometimes called rational intuition in discerning the necessary truths of mathematics. If so, then rational intuition should be included in the base set. But it is at least open to doubt whether rational intuition would score very high with regard to the practical virtues listed above. It doesn't seem the sort of thing that is necessarily correctable by other methods; and even if it is, it doesn't seem to have the virtue of publicity, at least to any great degree. Rational intuition seems to be a private affair.

How to handle such cases? Two suggestions come to mind. First, we might wax conservative, and argue that we should privilege, on Parallel Earth, all and only those fundamental principles that

(a) are either in the base set or give weight to those in the base set,

and

(b) would have more practical value than alternatives.

Call the set of principles that would meet these two condi-tions the *extended base set*. The methods of "natural instinct," such as observation and logic, would presumably belong here.

But it is far from clear, as already noted, that a principle recommending rational intuition would. From the conservative viewpoint, so much the worse for rational intuition. But this viewpoint may prove too limiting, for we may well see it as being in our collective best interest, in the long run, to allow those who have a developed palate (whether for modals or Malbec) to employ some methods that are closed to the rest of us. It seems more plausible, therefore, to go a more liberal route and adopt an "epistemic difference principle" of sorts. With our above criterion for practical value in hand, here is a rough formulation.

Epistemic Difference:   A fundamental principle outside of the extended base set should be privileged only if not privileging the principle would lower the total practical value of the members of the extended base set.

The thrust of this section has been to propose a strategy for answering skepticism about reason and, in particular, the problems that arise when our epistemic principles threaten to be incommensurable. That problem, at root, is a challenge to whether our fundamental epistemic commitments can be defended by reason. According to the strategy proposed here, they can. Our epistemic commitments can be defended as practically rational just when they are commitments to principles that we would have the most reason to employ in a hypothetical situation of epistemic and social equality. In short, we can rationally defend our epistemic principles just when they would win the method game.

These are reasons that appear to meet both constraints we laid down earlier. First, they are reasons that don't beg epistemic questions. At least hypothetically, we can give these reasons to each other in order to resolve deep epistemic disagreements. If that sounds quixotic, keep in mind the goal. The point isn't to find a bunch of bullet-points that could serve as the basis for a marketing campaign on behalf of reason ("Reason: good for what ails ya"). The point has been to demonstrate that we in fact already possess the common currency of reason. That common currency is grounded in the naturalness and practical rationality of the principles that are constitutive of public reason. If that is right, and the argument above suggests that it is, then it just falls out that skepticism about reason is mistaken: we *can* defend our fundamental epistemic commitments from a common point of view. And that, in turn, means that we can also understand our own changes in epistemic point of view as rational. We can give reasons to ourselves and to others for why we favor the epistemic principles we do.

Second, these are reasons that we can abstract from our immediate preferences. These reasons hold up whether we are Christians or atheists, Republicans or Democrats. What the above thought experiment shows, in other words, is that there are reasons to trust certain methods over others *even if* those methods run counter to your own worldview and the robust preferences that come with it. The ground for these reasons is nothing more than rational self-interest. In the "epistemic original position" (to adapt Rawls's phrase), where you don't know which methods are going to be reliable, your best bet, from your own perspective, is to trust (or privilege) those principles and methods which have the most practical value, which are part of our natural instincts, which we can't help but use, or which satisfy the epistemic difference principle. Which methods are these? Those that on balance can be used to generate objective, public reasons—the methods recommended by the principles of scientific reason. That, in short, is our two-step argument. It is practically rational to privilege open epistemic principles; the fundamental epistemic principles underlying science are open; so it is rational to privilege the fundamental epistemic principles of science.

## 4   Questions and Answers

Our two-step argument, and the method game in particular, raises some further questions. I won't be able to answer all of these questions in thoroughgoing detail here; but where I can, I'll gesture at how more complete answers might unfold.

*Q.   How do you know which principles will win the method game?*

I have not argued for a list of specific fundamental principles, nor would I try to do so. We can appeal to too many different and very specific epistemic principles to make that kind of list practical. What I have argued for is *a procedure for identifying reasons to commit to fundamental principles*. The principles that win will be those principles concerning methods that have, on balance and to a greater degree, a greater share of practical virtues—virtues that scientific methods happen to have. My point is that those methods already possess virtues, over and above their reliability for getting at the truth, which would make them particularly appealing to people in a hypothetical state of social and epistemic equality.

Might there not be other fundamental principles that could win out as well? It's possible. But there are some principles we've discussed that I think are unlikely to win. Consider the principle floated by our fictional young-earth creationist in chapter 3, that the most reliable method for learning about the distant past is consulting the Bible. Someone who already thinks this principle is true might be inclined to want to privilege it on Parallel Earth during rounds of the method game. But if they are (as we've stipulated) to play the game fairly, they can't argue that we should do so on the grounds that it is true or that God says that it is so. Nor can they plausibly make the case that it is forged from our natural instincts, like observation. For all we know, all of us playing the game may be unable to read or may not possess books on Parallel Earth. What they would have to argue is that consulting the Bible has as much or more practical value than appealing to competing principles such as PAST. And that will be extremely difficult. For PAST gives weight to methods already privileged by inclusion into the base set: observation, abduction, induction. Moreover, it is hardly clear, as I've already argued, that consultation of the Bible—at least when it is about what happened in the past—has the open character that makes other principles practically rational. It is difficult to see, in short, how we can judge that someone is consulting the Bible correctly on questions to which it does not give a single and unequivocal answer. Which passages should be given more weight than others? Which methods of interpretation should be used? The fact that there is so much debate about these questions, even among those who would privilege the method as such, suggests that on the scale of practical virtue, this method would not rank particularly high—even if, somehow, it turned out to be the most reliable.

Q. *The method game is unrealistic. Moreover, it asks us to abstract from the principles and preferences that are constitutive of our identity.*

The method game is a thought experiment, and so is by definition "unrealistic." The point of a thought experiment is to abstract from certain features of a possible situation so as to be able to focus the mind on other features. That is what the method game allows us to do: it allows us to think about how we would choose between epistemic principles in abstraction from both our actual social preferences and from the truth or falsity of those principles.

It is worth emphasizing here that the method game is, in an important respect, quite distinct from Rawls's original position. Rawls asked us to conceive of the people in the original position as something like "minimal selves"—people without social political and religious commitments. Not surprisingly, one of the most important and early lines of criticism of Rawls was that such minimal selves were stripped of the very commitments that made decision-making possible for people. Whether or not this criticism against Rawls is successful, the method game does not make the assumptions that engendered it. As I laid out the game, the people making the decisions—the game's players—are just like you and me. They come to the table with all the social and epistemic commitments that anyone might have. And they are entitled to rely on those commitments in making their decisions, during the game, about which principles to privilege on Parallel Earth. They just have to do so in accord with the game's rules. That is, players can (and doubtless will) use their social, moral, and epistemic commitments in making their decisions about which principles to privilege. But they can't assume (a) that they will have the same social and political commitments on Parallel Earth, or (b) that any of the epistemic principles they are relying on in the actual world will be true on Parallel Earth. In short, then, the players of the method game are not minimal selves. Their selves are as robust as yours and mine.

*Q. The method game requires us to form beliefs about epistemic principles, but you just noted that we would employ epistemic principles in doing so. Won't the players disagree about those principles too—making the game useless as a procedure for identifying reasons for principles?*

Keeping some distinctions in mind can mollify this worry.[22] On the one hand, there is the task the players are charged with: determining which principles to privilege on Parallel Earth. The rules of the game determine what sorts of reasons they can and can't appeal to in reaching their decisions. But of course, on the other hand, in reaching their decisions, the players will be committed to certain principles that favor some methods and sources over others. Imagine we are playing the game, and discussing whether consulting a given holy book is a method that should be privileged on Parallel Earth. In assessing your reasons, I will employ certain methods. I'll have reasons for thinking those methods are reliable in the actual world. But having reasons for a method's reliability in the actual world is completely consistent with *suspending judgment about whether those same methods will be reliable in some other world.* Consequently, even if you reject my methods and principles in the actual world (because you deem them unreliable), it does not follow that you can't agree with my assessments of what methods should be employed in a hypothetical position of epistemic equality.

Of course, it is possible that I will disagree with you, here on earth, over whether method M would have practical value on Parallel Earth. Moreover, it is possible that my disagreement with you will be due to the fact that you have used a method R, which I disapprove of, in reaching your decision about M's practical value on Parallel Earth. In other words, we may disagree over the methods we use in reaching our assessments of what would have practical value in our hypothetical situation of epistemic equality. How would we resolve such a debate? By playing the method game, naturally: we can play the game with regard to R just as well as we can play it with regard to M. If R wins, then I should acknowledge that it is a rational method to employ to figure out whether M itself wins the method game. This may prove to be complex; arguments about rationality mostly are. But there is no vicious regress. Indeed, given that we are finite creatures with finite methods of belief-formation, there cannot be. We will eventually run out of methods to quarrel about.

Q.  *Not everyone will be willing to "play" the method game*
*because it presupposes certain values that not everyone will share.*

The method game does presuppose some values. It presupposes, for example, that, given the opportunity, people would make decisions based on practical reason. To make decisions based on practical reason in the sense I intend here, is to be able to give reasons for one's actions, to think about one's own self-interest, to form a conception of the good, and to engage in critical reflection on one's life. If you don't know your future social position on Parallel Earth, for example, the method game predicts that you will not privilege principles whose effectiveness can only be judged by the socially privileged. You won't do so simply because that would not be practical, given what we might call one's *wide* self-interest—that is, one's self-interest in developing a life-plan and promoting the welfare of one's dependents.

Most people are willing to listen to reasons that appeal to what is in one's wide self-interest. This is so even if, as most people think, their wide self-interest is not their only value. Of course, this is not true of everyone. Some people will put much less stock in reasons that appeal to their wide self-interest than the rest of us. A person who thinks, for example, that it is evil to put their loved ones or themselves before the community as a whole might be unwilling to countenance the sort of practical reasons that will be generated by the method game. Of course, that does not mean that such a person will be deaf to the reasons we've adduced for privileging the principles constituting what I called the base set. And they may well see the practical value of appealing to open principles, not on the grounds of wide self-interest, but because it will be better for society as a whole. Of course, there may be some people who never, or almost never, act out of their own wide self-interest (such people would presumably be very short-lived). If so, then that shows what we already know to be the case: there is no rational magic bullet. There is no one reason that will convince everyone, *no matter what their values, commitments, or psychology*, of what is right or sensible. You don't need a philosopher to tell you that. But the fact that practical reasons of the sort I'm recommending won't convince everyone doesn't mean that they won't convince anyone. The strategy of the method game is to be as inclusive as possible. The structure of the game itself seeks some common ground that most human beings share, a common interest in the welfare and life-plans of its players and others close to them. It is on this basis that it argues that certain fundamental epistemic commitments are more rational than others, therefore providing a non-question-begging way of resolving deep epistemic disagreements. Some epistemic principles can be justified from a widely shared common point of view, that of our wide self-interest. If you aren't committed to the values that constitute that common point of view, then it is fair to say that our disagreements go far beyond the epistemic.

*Q.  The skeptical argument challenges us to defend our*
*fundamental epistemic commitments. But the method game gives*
*us only practical reasons for those commitments—and one might*
*think that offers stone instead of bread.*

It is certainly true that the method game does not supply us
with an intrinsically epistemic reason for epistemic principles.
That is, it doesn't give us a reason to believe any particular
principle is *true*. It is also not meant to; the skeptical argument
shows that I *can't give* epistemic reasons for fundamental epistemic principles to someone who doubts these principles. But
nevertheless I can, if the method game's strategy is correct, give
reasons for committing to those principles. And while these
reasons are not intrinsically epistemic, they do have *significant*
*epistemic consequences*.

First, recall that commitments in general have epistemic
consequences. To commit to P is to adopt a plan of using P as
a premise in your reasoning, of acting and theorizing on the
basis of P. Commitment to P means that further inquiry into
the truth of P stops (although it may, of course, be reopened in
the face of new data); to commit to P's truth is thus to treat the
matter as settled. Thus any commitment has epistemic consequences, because any commitment will have further implications for what else you might believe in, commit to, and do.

This point is magnified when the commitments in question
are themselves about matters epistemic. A commitment to a
fundamental epistemic principle is a commitment to the reliability (or the comparative reliability) of a particular method of
belief. Again, this isn't just to make an assumption. To commit
to an epistemic principle is to employ the method and *to treat*
*it as reliable for forming beliefs*. And to treat a method of belief-
formation as reliable in your daily life is to trust that method,

and therefore its results—the beliefs it produces.[23] Being committed to epistemic principles thus means being willing to employ a given method of belief, and hence, if I take myself as rational in employing the method then I take myself as rational in holding the beliefs it produces. And this means that if we show, via the method game, that it is rational to commit to a fundamental principle, we've also shown that it is rational to trust the method in question. Arguably then, if a method of belief-formation is trustworthy, it is also rational to hold the beliefs it produces, since beliefs that are produced by trustworthy methods are prima facie rational. Consequently, if those beliefs turn out to be true, and rational true belief constitutes knowledge, then we can say that the propositions believed by these methods are known. Thus winning the method game has epistemic consequences.[24]

This is not the only type of epistemic consequence my strategy here may have. Arguably, a society that privileged winning epistemic principles would be epistemically better off than one that did not. I've argued that the principles that would win the method game would be open and objective. As the philosopher Michael Fuerstein has also pointed out, a commitment to open and objective epistemic principles is a prerequisite for epistemic trust, and epistemic trust is likely to lead to a greater amount of knowledge across society as a whole.[25]

None of us can be experts in everything; indeed, few of us can be experts in anything. We are too busy and there is too much to know; life is short. So in order to get around in the world—to drive a safe car, to live in a house with electricity, to have one's illnesses addressed—we must trust that other people *do* know what they are talking about. That is, we must feel that we have rational grounds to commit to at least some of what others tell us about their areas of expertise. Yet if I am going to do that—if I am going to have faith that you know what you claim to know—then my faith can't be blind. I have to have some sense that your methods of knowing are reliable. Where your methods are opaque to the outside world, the rest of us have no way of verifying whether you do know what you are talking about. The same will be true of you, of course, if the situation is reversed. Consequently, epistemic trust—the sort of trust we engage in every day by using and employing the ordinary technological means of our society—is bolstered by reliance on open, objective epistemic principles.

Call this the argument from epistemic trust: The more objective and open a principle is, the more we will trust the results achieved from using the method it recommends. The more we trust each other's methods, the more likely it is that our knowledge will increase across society as a whole. Thus, the more we employ open and objective principles, the greater chance we have of increasing our knowledge.

In one sense, this argument from epistemic trust provides us with independent epistemic reasons to favor the principles of reason. Committing to these principles appears likely to increase our knowledge via increasing our epistemic trust in each other. Of course, in the context of skepticism about our fundamental epistemic principles, it is unclear that such an argument could be used to *give* an epistemic reason for our epistemic principles without begging the question against whoever is questioning those principles. The method game, however, does supply non-question-begging reasons to privilege open and objective epistemic principles. Thus, the two arguments are complimentary. The argument from epistemic trust tells us that adopting such principles is likely to result in an increase in knowledge across society as a whole. Therefore, we can conclude that winning the method game has epistemic consequences: the adoption of those principles that win the game, insofar as they are open and objective, is likely to increase knowledge across society as a whole.

Doubtless some will still pine for intrinsically epistemic reasons for our fundamental epistemic principles. It is worth stressing that nothing I've said here implies that you can't have them. As I have already pointed out, the skeptical argument doesn't prevent you from *having* epistemic reasons to believe your fundamental epistemic principles. What the skeptical argument shows is that we can't *exchange* such reasons with someone who challenges our principles.

If we want to exchange reasons for our foundational epistemic principles, we need to exchange practical reasons. Indeed, we ought to. If you and I are involved in a deep disagreement over epistemic principles, and yet we are to engage in real discussion, we should respect each other as fellow judgers—as alike in being capable of arriving at the truth. And where we respect each other as fellow judgers, we *should*, whenever possible, defend our claims with reasons that we can *both* recognize as reasons. And if we are to satisfy the demand to respect each other as fellow judgers, we should appeal to some common currency of reasons in justifying even our epistemic commitments. For only by doing so can we give reasons that can be recognized as reasons.

Committing is, in an obvious sense, more difficult than passive belief. Commitment, whether to another person or an epistemic principle, is a risk, and brings with it the possibility of failure and disappointment. It entails a willingness to act— in the present context, a willingness to employ the relevant method or methods for forming beliefs. So while the strategy set out here doesn't produce noncircular evidence for the fundamental principles of reason—and no strategy could, if the skeptical argument is sound—it does give us reasons for doing what is arguably more difficult: committing to those principles. Moreover, as the point about epistemic trust suggests, these reasons remain indirectly relevant to knowledge. When we aim at knowledge, we aim to believe more truths than falsehoods. It is surely relevant to discover that certain commitments—namely, those that would win the method game—are the most rational to have in pursuit of that goal.

# 6  Truth and the Pathos of Distance

## 1  A Picture of Knowledge

A ubiquitous picture of the academy divides it into "two cultures," to use C. P. Snow's familiar phrase. One culture, the sciences, is in the business of acquiring objective knowledge, of telling us the truth about the world. The other culture, the arts and humanities, is in the business of doing, well, something else. Just what else is hard to say—broadening the imagination, analyzing concepts, transforming our sense of difference. These answers all have merit; but despite that merit and their air of gravitas, the traditional picture of the two cultures has had the effect of making the humanities something of a second-class citizen in the eyes of the public, and at times in the eyes of academics themselves. After all, the picture implies that whatever else we may be doing, we humanist intellectuals aren't aiming at truth; we aren't producing knowledge.

The "two-culture" view can make the arguments I've advanced in this book on behalf of reason seem self-defeating. The reasons I've given on behalf of reason come from the humanities—they are philosophical, political, and moral reasons. I've claimed, in particular, that we have practical—that is, moral and political—reasons to privilege the fundamental epistemic principles of science in our society. But if, as the two-culture view implies, our moral and political arguments aren't even capable of being true, then why take them seriously? Indeed, the two-culture view can make the thesis of this book seem quixotic. You can't defend reason with reasons that aren't true.

Of course, not everyone accepts the idea of these "two cultures." Indeed, the unhappily named "postmodern" movements that blossomed at the end of the last century could be seen as a response to it. Postmodern theory is one version of a type of a "leveling-down" strategy we have seen elsewhere in the book. The basic idea of such strategies is to take the principles of scientific rationality to be on the same "level" as other principles. One version we've seen emerges from the political Right: if our commitment to scientific principles of rationality is just another faith, then science itself is no better, epistemically speaking, than religion. Here, the idea is that there is no such thing as objective truth, so the humanities are no worse off than the sciences.

Although he despised the label "postmodernist," the late Richard Rorty was one the most influential and intelligent proponents of this response. As Rorty saw matters, a major cause of our infatuation with this bad picture of knowledge is a misguided allegiance to what philosophers call "realism," or the view, roughly, that truth depends not on us but on how things are in the world. As Robert Brandom has noted, Rorty's master idea is that realism is the philosopher's secular religion. Like religion proper, it is the incarnation of the "pathos of distance" or the sense that there is a nonhuman Reality to which our thoughts and claims are responsible. Like belief in God, which often encourages the thought that only priests can tell us the important truths about the world, Rorty takes realism to encourage the thought that, in Sellars's words, "science is the measure of all things." As Rorty puts the point:

Nowadays the role once played by defenders of religious belief is played by defenders of realism . . . [who believe that] the natural sciences are in touch with The Intrinsic Nature of Reality, and perhaps no other portion of culture is. In their view, people who do not accept this answer are undermining civilization as we know it (the same view that Wilberforce took of T. H. Huxley). Such people lack humility, they lack respect for non-human reality. To have this humility is to grant the knowledge-claims of the natural scientist a special character— "objectivity" or "objective truth."[1]

Rorty's response to this realist picture of knowledge and science is to dismiss the idea of "objective" truth as a chimera. For Rorty, like Dewey and James before him, beliefs are better or worse not in virtue of how they agree with reality, but in virtue of how they help us to accomplish our goals. As we saw in chapter 3, Rorty embraces, with Kuhn and Foucault, a picture of science that sees it as "one more human activity, rather than as the place at which human beings encounter a 'hard' nonhuman reality." Of course, this is not meant to denigrate science; Rorty is a naturalist and no silly science-basher. Science is a human activity, but it is an extremely *important and valuable* human activity, one that can help us accomplish many of our goals better than any other method. But the goals that science helps us reach are not to be described in terms of "getting us closer to the truth" or to "the nature of reality":

No area of culture, and no period of history, gets Reality more right than any other. The difference between areas and epochs is their relative efficiency at accomplishing various purposes.[2]

As Rorty sees matters, we would be immeasurably better off giving up on our sense of humility in the face of a nonhuman reality and the associated idea that our thoughts are true when they correspond to that reality. Giving up on the pathos of distance is giving up on the idea that humanity shivers in a cave from which only the Other—be it the Good, or God, or Reality-in-Itself—can free us. To give up on the realist's idea of truth is therefore a liberating act, a step forward in world-historical human development. It means that we can stop worrying about which beliefs get at the objective truth and start worrying about which beliefs are useful for making us better human beings. It means that we are growing up and accepting full responsibility for ourselves, no longer abasing ourselves before the illusory authority of the nonhuman.

I agree with Rorty that the hackneyed "two-cultures" picture of knowledge and the academy should be rejected, and that a commitment to "naturalism" doesn't mean that we have to say that the sciences have an exclusive contract with reality. On this issue at least, Rorty and I (and Wright, Price, and Putnam, among other heroes of mine) are on the same side, while many analytic philosophers are on the other. Moreover, I agree with Rorty that debates over realism are often carried on with religious fervor. And I also agree that when passion replaces argument—and the topic is metaphysics!—this is as good a sign as any that certain basic assumptions need rethinking.

But I can't go along with Rorty's alternative picture. For that alternative amounts to the intellectual equivalent of destroying the village in order to save it. It defends the humanities from the charge that they can't tell us the objective truth by denying that there is any objective truth in the first place.

As I hope to indicate in what follows, this strategy is a mistake, both metaphysically and politically. Rorty is right that we must rethink our assumptions about truth. But the assumption we need to rethink is not that truth is "objective," nor that inquiry is aimed at truth, but rather an assumption that Rorty shares with his realist opponents. This assumption is that truth either has a single "nature" (and that this nature consists in "correspondence to Reality") or that it has no nature at all. To reject this assumption is to entertain the idea that not only may the humanities and the sciences have different ways of getting at the truth, but that the truths they get at may differ in kind.

In this chapter, I address three connected points. The first is an argument against the idea that no sort of rational inquiry—scientific, humanistic or otherwise—is aimed at the truth. The second concerns the kind of truth that seems the aim of at least some parts of the humanities. The third concerns why, *pace* Rorty, this kind of truth still can be, and indeed needs to be, connected to a natural world beyond our own creation.

## 2  Truth and Inquiry

According to Rorty, the social practice of giving reasons to each other neither needs nor requires what he considered the "transcendent" goal of truth. The only thing that transcends a social practice, Rorty thinks, is another social practice. As such, it doesn't help to say that truth is the aim of such practices:

I know how to aim at greater honesty, greater charity, greater patience, greater inclusiveness and so on. I see democratic politics as serving such concrete, describable goals. But I do not see that it helps to add "truth" . . . to our list of goals, for I do not see what we shall do differently if such additions are made.[3]

Consequently, the question of truth is irrelevant to democratic politics, because, as he makes clear:

The grounding premise of my argument is that you cannot aim at something, cannot work to get it, unless you can recognize it once you have got it. . . . We shall never know for sure whether a given belief is true, but we can be sure that nobody is presently able to summon up any residual objections to it, that everybody agrees that it ought to be held.[4]

The argument here is essentially this: Truth cannot be the target of our justificatory practices—of inquiry, so to speak—because we can never know whether our beliefs are true. And a target we can't know we've hit is no target at all. Yet we can know whether "everybody agrees" with a belief. Therefore, agreement or consensus, not truth, is the proper aim of inquiry.

This argument is curious on a number of fronts. First, why *isn't* it possible for me to know whether my beliefs are true? Well, skeptical arguments against knowledge might be one reason. Such arguments say that if we can't rule out the possibility that we are mistaken, we don't know what we think we know. But if that is the sort of skepticism that is driving Rorty's argument (and I don't think it is), then it becomes even more curious why we should think that we *can* know for sure that "everybody agrees" that a certain belief "ought to be held." What about *this* is so immune from doubt? Indeed, for most beliefs that I am sure are true, I am not at all sure that everyone agrees they are true. After all, "everyone"—even if it is just "everyone in my culture," or even "everyone in my culture who looks and speaks like me"—includes quite a lot of folks. Figuring out that "everyone agrees" with me in regard to even the most mundane beliefs is not easy.

A second point to make about this argument is that it assumes a mistaken picture of how justification (reason-giving) is related to truth. In general, we can distinguish between the ultimate end or value that *governs* a practice and the more immediate aims that are justified because they are means to this end. The former is the light, however faint, by which the practice steers, so to speak; the latter are the more immediate reference-points practitioners may take to move them along their way. In saying that true belief is a goal of inquiry, we take it to be an aim of inquiry in the first sense. One thing we can agree with Rorty about is that an individual inquirer rarely has anything so fancy as truth as a conscious aim in her everyday life. And even when she does, she cannot achieve that end directly. One does not simply will oneself to believe. Rather, we pursue truth indirectly, by pursuing evidence that supplies us with reasons for belief. Indirectly or not, however, it is truth that supplies the point of this enterprise, and what distinguishes it from merely pursuing that which will rally others to our cause, or flatter our opinions. Reasons for a belief are *reasons* because they are means to the further end of truth. Thus justification (reason-giving) is distinct from truth precisely as a means is distinct from its end.

Rorty sometimes seems to concede that there is a point here. But he thinks that all it amounts to is that the word "true" has what he calls a "cautionary" use. We use the word in this way, he thinks, to remind ourselves that what may be justified to one audience may not be justified to another, or "to remind oneself that there might be . . . objections that have not occurred to any one."[5] It is certainly good to remind ourselves of this fact. But the reason I think it is good is because some of those objections might turn out to be right, and my view may turn out to be wrong. Admitting that we can be wrong is admitting that what we believe is the case, and what we can justify to each other as being the case, needn't *be* the case. This is a fact about truth and justification.

Rorty was no skeptic, however. At heart, I think he had a different argument in mind: It is impossible to ever hit the target of truth, not because of skeptical interference, but because the target itself is fundamentally flawed. His point is that the sense in which we might think that truth is the goal of reason and justification is a dubious, metaphysical sense of truth. It involves, as he elsewhere makes clear, a commitment to a looking-glass view of the mind, a view according to which our thoughts, when correct, are mirrors of nature. In short, Rorty thinks that the conception of reason and justification I've been defending in this book assumes an objectionable correspondence theory of truth. And Rorty's point is not just that we couldn't know whether our beliefs correspond to the world, but that this should show us that the entire notion of truth as correspondence is unhelpful.

This is a better argument—more interesting, and more plausible. It makes an important point. But it overstates the case. The problem isn't so much with the correspondence idea of truth as with the idea that this is the only kind of truth there is.

## 3   Representing the World

Beliefs are true when the world is as they portray it to be, when they correspond to the facts. This is a truism. And like all truisms, it only goes so far. As Simon Blackburn has remarked, "we do not raise the theoretical temperature very far if we substitute 'corresponds to the facts' for 'says of what is that it is.'"[6] The problem is that when we do say something more about these matters, we run the risk of saying that 'truth' consists in something that philosophical and humanistic judgments could never achieve. The reason for this is that the most promising contemporary theories of correspondence emerge out of the representational theory of mind currently dominating cognitive science.

The view of truth that falls out of such theories is that truth is accurate representation. Thus, a belief—understood here as a mental state that supervenes on some network of brain states—is true when things are as the belief represents them as being. Roughly, beliefs represent states of affairs in the same way that a road map represents the highway system.[7] In order for a map to be accurate, the map and what it maps must share a common structure: the bits of the map must display the same relations to each other that bits of the landscape display. Map and landscape are isomorphic, and not accidentally so: an accurate map wouldn't be the way it is unless the landscape it maps had the structure it has. Similarly, we can say that a belief is true when it maps—is causally isomorphic with—some obtaining state of affairs.[8]

Such theories, promising or not, are most plausible when applied to the sorts of conclusions we reach in the sciences. The metaphor of the map shows why. You can't map what isn't there, and you can't map well that to which you bear no causal relationship—no matter how indirect. In a bumper sticker: *if we are to correspond, we must respond.* Where we have some thought about Xs but responsiveness fails, either because we aren't plausibly in contact with any Xs or there simply are no Xs, then a representationalist account seems to be ruled out.

Consider, for example, any of the following claims:

The murder of innocents is wrong.

Torturing a prisoner is a violation of that person's rights.

We ought to privilege the fundamental epistemic principles of science.

Take, in particular, the proposition that torturing a prisoner is a violation of his human rights. Under the assumption that truth is always and everywhere causal mapping, it is a vexing question how this thought *could* be true. That torture is a violation of a right is certainly plausible, but do we really think it can only be true if there are extralegal (if not extra-institutional) entities that exist in the physical world, jostling around with the rest of the objects that clutter the universe? How could such entities causally interact with us? In short, if we were to understand all truth as accurate representation of natural objects, it is not clear how such claims could be in the running for truth or falsity. It is unclear because it is hard to see how rightness and wrongness are independent properties of actions mapped by our brains.

A long tradition in analytic philosophy has it that since truth *is* always and everywhere accurate representation, and moral and political claims can't be true in that way, we must conclude that such claims aren't capable of being true. They may be good for something else—self-expression or political manipulation, say—but a claim like "Torture is wrong" isn't really true. Indeed, a view like this is pretty common in our culture—and not just among philosophers. Rorty and I both find it somewhat depressing and misguided. But it is worth noting that this response also threatens to be self-undermining. For the claim that certain sorts of propositions are not apt for correspondence-style truth is itself a philosophical claim, and *philosophical claims are hardly ideal candidates for mapping external reality as it is in itself.* If we are to be skeptical about the truth-aptness of certain claims in the humanities, we had better start with philosophical claims. But that itself is a philosophical claim, and anyone who bothers to make it presumably would think it is true.

For this reason, among others, I think that we are already committed to taking many of our philosophical beliefs as being at least capable of being true.[9] Some will shrug and conclude that this just means that every belief is capable of being true in a thoroughly thin, deflationary sense. To say that the propositional content of a belief is true, on such accounts, is not to ascribe some interesting property to that proposition, but—at least in most cases—simply to assert that proposition by other means.[10] Hence, as Rorty once put it, truth, is "not the sort of thing we should expect to have a philosophically interesting theory about."[11]

This deflationary gambit has its merits, but I don't find it particularly persuasive. Some of my reasons for rejecting it, which I've given elsewhere, are particular to the details of the deflationary position.[12] My most basic reason for not accepting deflationism, however, is simply this: at its heart, deflationism is a negative program. It rests on the assumption that traditional views of truth—views like the correspondence theory of truth— face counterexamples like the ones just raised. But to throw in the towel just because of these problems is to buy into the same tired dilemma that I noted earlier: either one and only one property makes propositions true—or nothing does.

I see no good reason to grant this assumption. It simply overlooks a more interesting alternative: that there is more than one property, something besides correspondence to the facts that makes our beliefs true. As I've argued elsewhere, to understand what truth is, you must understand what it does. Truth is a functional notion, and truths are what they are because they play a particular role. Thus, if we want to ask about what kind of truth philosophical and theoretical claims are apt for, we should ask: What property plays the truth-role for such judgments?[13] Once we see that when we are talking about truth we are talking about a particular job or functional role, we can see the mistake in assuming that there is one and only one way for judgments (or their contents) to be true. It opens up the possibility that there is more than one property that plays the truth-role. It opens up, in other words, the possibility of making sense of *pluralism about truth*.

## 4    Truth and the Human

Wilfrid Sellars famously defined philosophy as the attempt to say how things, in the widest sense of the term, hang together, in the widest sense of the term. Even if, in other fields, we aren't always casting the widest net possible, as we are in philosophy, Sellars' core thought—that in inquiry we wish to understand how things "hang together"—captures something deeply right about what we are striving to do, not just in philosophy but in many of the humanistic disciplines, including political theory and economics. At least some of the time, we aren't aiming to represent objects out in the world. We are aiming to weave the information we have into a coherent whole that withstands theoretical pressure.

But it is one thing to think that coherence is a sign of truth. Could it sometimes also constitute truth? On the face of it, the answer seems to be "No." As we've already noted, truth is not justification or warrant. Being true is a more objective property of beliefs. In the present context this means, first, that the truth of a belief isn't just due to its being a belief. Believing doesn't make it so. Likewise, it can't just depend on whether we have evidence for that proposition here and now. So if property X is going to play the truth-role, it must be possible for some beliefs to be X at a given time without being warranted at that time, and it must be possible for some beliefs to be warranted without being X. Given these truisms, we obviously don't want to say that what makes beliefs about human rights true, or what makes epistemic commitments the ones we should have, is that they are merely coherent. What is coherent today may not be so tomorrow, and the mere fact that some explanation hangs together right now doesn't mean it is true. Lots of crazy ideas hang together.

But, following the lead of Peirce, Putnam, and Crispin Wright, we might say that such judgments are true when they are coherent *in a very strong sense*—a sense already pointed toward by Rorty, above—that is, by being durably coherent in the face of new information and constant debate. Such durable coherence is not a plausible candidate for what makes every true proposition true, but it might be a plausible candidate for what makes some propositions true. Let's say that a belief is *supercoherent* if and only if it would be a member of a coherent system of beliefs at some stage of inquiry and remain so *in every successive stage of inquiry*.[14] The point here is that some beliefs might end up being true not because of how they represent the world as being but because we never encounter any reason to give them up. They always fit with the evidence and our other beliefs no matter what twists and turns experience may bring us.[15] Supercoherence is eternal, undefeated coherence.

Supercoherence is much harder to achieve than mere coherence. So it is more plausible as a contender for playing the truth-role. It has, as we might put it, all the marks of truth. First, supercoherence is distinct from mere warrant: a judgment can be warranted by the evidence at some stage of inquiry but not supercoherent, or it can be supercoherent but not warranted right now. Second, the possibility for error is ample: just because everyone I know justifiably believes some proposition doesn't mean that it is supercoherent. Third, as defined, supercoherence is a stable notion: if a proposition is supercoherent, then it is supercoherent at any stage of inquiry. And fourth, supercoherence has the relevant normative import for belief that truth has: it could hardly fail to be valuable to believe what is supercoherent.

So supercoherence looks promising as a contender for playing the truth-role for beliefs of certain kinds. But it can't be the whole story. In commenting on a previous attempt of mine to articulate this suggestion, Rorty himself points us to the reason why:

[According to Lynch] if you cannot find an object in the world that makes a given belief true, coherence—in the form of ideal assertibility—will do the truth-making job just as well. So we do not have to do any ontological heavy lifting to find appropriate truth-makers for beliefs (such as those about human rights) whose relation to the world has struck philosophers as problematic. . . . But if coherence will do in morals (and presumably in mathematics, and in various other areas) why not everywhere? If ideal coherence is all the objectivity you need in morals, why should it not be enough in particle physics?[16]

Put in the present terms, Rorty's question is: If supercoherence can do the job of truth for the sorts of claims we make in the humanities, then why not everywhere? I answer: Supercoherence can't do the job of truth anywhere unless it *doesn't* do the job everywhere. The basic reason for this is simple. Unless there are facts about what *makes* a belief-system coherent or incoherent—and facts that don't consist in supercoherence—then there is nothing to nail down that system. It will float free of reality. What makes a system S supercoherent, for example, can't just be that "S is supercoherent" supercoheres with S. That would be like saying that systems are supercoherent just when they say they are. So unless some truths are true by virtue of something *other* than supercoherence, supercoherence is not a very plausible contender for doing the job of truth.[17]

The upshot is that supercoherence is not a plausible candidate for what makes our moral and political beliefs true (if they are ever lucky enough to be so). Even if the truth of some beliefs is explained in terms of supercoherence, the truth of all beliefs cannot be.[18] Just because our story says our story is coherent doesn't make it so.

So even if we agree with philosophers like Rorty that certain kinds of inquiry are in the business of constructing coherent, narrative explanations and systems of belief, we can't avoid the pathos of distance. We can't avoid nailing our beliefs down to something that is not narrative, something external, something that lies at a distance. If we want to say that truth is to be found in the misty forests of the humanities, we must say that truth does not always and everywhere manifest itself in the same way.

What can serve to nail down our systems of beliefs? Two points seem relevant. First, as just suggested, one thing that makes our belief-systems supercoherent (if they happen to be) is an objective fact (or set of facts) about what is and isn't warranted, what is or isn't coherent.[19] Second, if membership in a durably coherent system is going to make a belief true, that system must not only be *internally* supercoherent, it must be eternally compatible with the *external* coherence-independent facts—with whatever kinds of beliefs are true, in other words, by virtue of corresponding to an extra-human reality. Thus no humanistic narrative, no matter how internally coherent or durable in the face of criticism, should convince us that skin color affects intelligence or that AIDS can be caught through sweat. For those kinds of beliefs aren't true or false because of their coherence or lack thereof, but because they represent or fail to represent objects and properties in the natural world.

Call a belief-system that meets both of these constraints—internal supercoherence and compatibility with external facts—*concordant*. My suggestion, in short, is that *we see certain kinds of inquiries, including our moral and philosophical inquiries, as aiming at constructing concordant explanations*. Such explanations, were there ever to be any, are systems of beliefs and commitments, some of which are true in virtue of corresponding to the facts but others of which—such as our philosophical and ethical beliefs—are true simply by being part of the explanation.

In making this suggestion, I am guilty of oversimplifying. Intellectuals, philosophers among them, aren't solely interested in constructing concordant explanations. We are also interested in self-expression, transformation, beauty, happiness—and sometimes we are only interested in these things, and couldn't care less about truth. And of course, sometimes our beliefs are not normative—not about what is good or bad, rational or irrational. But when they are, we are hoping to say what is true by saying what makes sense, what hangs together.

Some will worry that concordance is not objective enough. After all, they'll ask, what rules out the possibility that there might be two equally concordant, but inconsistent, systems of belief? That is, might there not be more than one narrative of "the history of human rights," for example, that would hold up equally well in the face of all future criticism, and accord equally well with all the relevant empirical facts both now and forever into the future? And might not these narratives be inconsistent to boot? Well, sure. But so what? The fact that there may be more than one true story of the world when it comes to such matters is hardly news (except to some philosophers). The important thing is that given the constraints on concordance, not every story is equally true: many will never make the cut.

Some will worry, to the contrary, that concordance is too objective. It only takes a moment to see that most of what we believe about political morality, or the basis of gender equality, or the nature of ethnic identity is probably not going to have the exalted status of concordance. To this I say: tough beans. I never promised a rose garden of easy knowledge. Knowledge requires truth, and truth is hard to come by.

The usual debates over truth confront us with a false dilemma: either all truth is correspondence or there is no truth at all. I've argued that there is a third way. If—and indeed, only if—we are willing to be pluralists about truth, we can understand some of our beliefs as true in virtue of concordance. And if that is so, then we are free to say what we already know—that our philosophical reasons, indeed our reasons in the humanities generally, are real reasons after all.

# Conclusion

Human beings have a tendency to throw the baby out with the bathwater. From the obvious fact that everything, including reason, has its limits, we are tempted toward skepticism about reason and its relevance to our lives. I have argued that this is a mistake, in two ways.

One way in which it is a mistake is philosophical. Philosophers have overblown the capacities of reason—both in celebrating its alleged role as ruler of the passions, and in its ability to justify itself. But we can give up these faulty assumptions about reason without giving up on the value of reason itself. We don't need to throw up our hands and say that everything is arbitrary.

Philosophers often contrast two pictures of how our beliefs are related. In one picture, our beliefs are like a building. Most of these beliefs, including those that inform our everyday life, compose the upper floors. But we often overlook others, which make up the lower floors and the very foundation itself, supporting all the rest. The other picture takes it that there simply are no fundamental principles, and thus there is no foundation. Rather, our beliefs form a reinforcing system. They are much more like a raft at sea, and we can only replace one belief by standing on others.

The view of reason defended in this book shares something with both of these pictures, but is ultimately different from either. The fundamental principles of reason are less like the foundation of a building and more like the keystone of an arch. Without the keystone, the arch cannot hold its weight and must collapse. It is not like a replaceable plank on a raft. But the keystone also cannot support the arch by itself. Other stones must also be in place; and we can never look to the keystone alone. So while I've argued that broadly scientific principles of rationality can be defended against skepticism both old and new, I haven't done so by appealing to self-justifying foundations. Instead, I've argued that we must defend our fundamental epistemic commitments with objective, practical reasons. Scientific rationality can be defended, in short, because it has virtues that are central to a just and civil society.

Giving up on reason isn't just a philosophical mistake. It is also a political mistake. Skepticism about reason encourages us to give up on the one really inspired idea of the Enlightenment, that we share a common currency of reason with our fellow human beings. And once we give up on the idea that there is a common point of view that is partly constituted by a commitment to shared principles distinguishing what is rational from what isn't, we also give up on the idea of a civil society. We'll just start thinking that conservatives and liberals can't really reasonably debate each other, that they rely on different kinds of reason.[1] And once we do that, we are a hop, skip and a jump away from regarding all of our political opponents as lunatics and idiots.[2] The currently poisonous political climate in the United States illustrates this slide with disturbing clarity. If there are no shared standards of rationality, then we are apt to think that it is not worth bothering to give and ask for reasons. We are apt to stop looking for truth and stick with what is convenient.

So I end with a caution and a hope. The caution is that if we slide much farther from a commitment to reason, we will find it impossible as a society to claw our way back. Thus my hope. I hope to live in a society that sees a difference between what pays and what is, between everyone believing something and its really being so, between what seems reasonable in the short term and what survives the fires of rational debate, between brute appeals to power and patient appeals to our better natures. I hope to live in a society, in short, that does not just passively accept reason but is passionately committed to it, that puts its principles into action.

# Notes

## 1 Hope and Reason

1. Kevin Trudeau, *Natural Cures: What "They" Don't Want You to Know About* (Alliance Publishing, 2006), p. 327. Among other things, Trudeau's book claims that we can change the structure of DNA just by thinking about it.

2. From a sample of 1,007 adults, aged 18 and older, conducted June 1–3, 2007. See Frank Newport, "Majority of Republicans Doubt Evolution," Gallup News Service, June 11, 2007.

3. According to an August 2006 survey from the Pew Forum on Religion and Public Life and the Pew Research Center for the People and the Press, 62 percent of respondents said that scientists agree on the validity of evolution; "Many Americans Uneasy with Mix of Religion and Politics," August 24, 2006, p. 16: http://pewforum.org/Politics-and -Elections/Many-Americans-Uneasy-with-Mix-of-Religion-and-Politics .aspx#3. But a Gallup poll from February 11, 2009 suggested that fewer than 4 in 10 Americans believe in evolution themselves. Frank Newport, "On Darwin's Birthday, Only 4 in 10 Believe in Evolution," *Gallup News Service*, February 11, 2009.

4. David Masci, "How the Public Resolves Conflicts Between Faith and Science," The Pew Forum on Religion and Public Life, August 27, 2007. Masci is referencing a *Time* magazine poll from October 2006.

5. Strictly, we can distinguish between sense-perception as such—the act of forming immediate beliefs by way of your senses, and what I am calling "observation"—the act of drawing inferences from sense-perception, consciously or not. The latter, but not the former, is generally not thought to employ your reason as such, but in normal adult human experience the two are inextricably intertwined.

6. Many philosophers have taken "reason" in a still narrower sense, to mean the ability to grasp that certain propositions are true independently of experience, or a priori. I have no quarrel with a priori reasoning per se; but in this book I am more interested in the sense of "reason" we have in mind when we think of scientific method as exemplifying reason.

7. See C. Dunbar, *One Nation Under God* (Oviedo, Fla.: Higher Life Development Services, 2008), Russell Shorto, "How Christian Were the Founders?" *New York Times Magazine* (February 11, 2010), pp. 32–47, and James C. Mckinley, Jr., "Texas Conservatives Seek Deeper Stamp on Texts," *New York Times*, March 10, 2010.

8. This is what the philosopher Paul Boghossian seems to suggest when he says, "[The claim] that we cannot hope to justify our principles through the use of those very principles is not true in general, it is true only in the special, albeit important case where we have *legitimately* come to doubt the correctness of our own principles." Paul Boghossian, *Fear of Knowledge* (Oxford: Oxford University Press, 2006), p. 100.

9. David Hume, *Enquiry Concerning the Principles of Morals* in *Enquires Concerning Human Understanding and Concerning the Principles of Morals*, 3rd ed., ed. L. A. Selby-Bigge, revised by P. H. Nidditch (Oxford: Oxford University Press, 1975), IX, 1, pp. 272–273. My invocation of Hume here is influenced by Simon Blackburn's discussion of the common point of view, and its relation to civility, in his *Ruling Passions* (Oxford: Oxford University Press, 1998), pp. 210–211. See also Rachel Cohen, "The Common Point of View in Hume's Ethics," *Philosophy and Phenomenological Research* 57 (1997): 827–850.

10. J. Cohen, "Deliberation and Democratic Legitimacy," in *Deliberative Democracy: Essays on Reason and Politics*, ed. J. Bohman and W. Rehg (Cambridge, Mass.: MIT Press, 1997), p. 72.

11. On "public reason," see John Rawls, *Political Liberalism* (New York: Columbia University Press, 1996), pp. 212–213. But where Rawls (p. 213) imbues public reasons with three functions, I am only emphasizing what he calls the "moral duty" of civility—the idea that we should aim to explain our views to each other by appeal to reasons that could, ideally, be accepted by all. For a nuanced criticism of the greater Rawlsian view on public reason, see Gerald Gaus, "Reason, Justification, and Consensus," in *Deliberative Democracy*, p. 214. See also Habermas's critique of Rawls: "Reconciliation Through the Public Use of Reason: Remarks on John Rawls's *Political Liberalism*," *Journal of Philosophy* 92 (1995): 109–131.

12. Jean Hampton, "Should Political Philosophy Be Done without Metaphysics?" *Ethics* 99 (1989): 791–814.

13. An important recent, if very different, defense of the idea that there are common epistemological principles is Robert Talisse's engaging *Democracy and Moral Conflict* (Cambridge: Cambridge University Press, 2009). Talisse argues that we in fact do possess certain common folk epistemological principles that we can appeal to in political disagreements. In contrast, I think we *should* have such principles in common. Chapter 5 gives the full-dress argument for why this is so.

14. Michael Oakeshott, *Rationalism in Politics and Other Essays* (Indianapolis: The Liberty Fund, 1991), p. 6.

### 2 Neither Slave nor Master: Reason and Emotion

1. A. Todorov, A. N. Mandisodza, A. Goren, and C. C. Hall, "Inferences of Competence from Faces Predict Election Outcomes," *Science* 308 (2005): 1623–1626; C. Ballew II and A. Todorov, "Predicting Political Elections from Rapid and Unreflective Judgments," *Proceedings of the National Academy of the Sciences* 104 (2007): 17948–17953.

2. Ballew II and Todorov, "Predicting Political Elections," p. 17951.

3. See in particular the work of Jonathan Haidt, e.g., J. Haidt, "The Emotional Dog and Its Rational Tail: A Social Intuitionist Approach to Moral Judgment," *Psychological Review* 108, no. 4 (2001): 814–834. See also J. Haidt, S. Koller, M. Dias, "Affect, Culture, and Morality, or Is It Wrong to Eat Your Dog?" *Journal of Personality and Social Psychology* 65 (1993): 613–628. Also helpful is Michael Gazzaniga's *Human: The Science Behind What Makes Us Unique* (New York: Harper Perennial, 2008). Paul Bloom, in a recent issue of *Nature*, has argued, as I do below, that reason plays a role in moral judgment; see Bloom, "How Do Morals Change?" *Nature* 464 (2010): 490. Two recent overviews by informed nonspecialists, both of whom argue that reason has less to do with our decisions than we might think, are Jonah Lehrer, *How We Decide* (New York: Houghton Mifflin, 2009), and David Brooks, *The Social Animal* (New York: Random House, 2011).

4. Drew Westen, Pavel S. Blagov, Keith Harenski, Clint Kilts, and Stephan Hamann, "Neural Bases of Motivated Reasoning: An fMRI Study of Emotional Constraints on Partisan Political Judgment in the 2004 U.S. Presidential Election," *Journal of Cognitive Neuroscience* 18, no. 11 (2006): 1947–1958.

5. *Phaedrus*, 246a–b, 253c ff. *Selected Dialogues of Plato*, trans. B. Jowett (New York: Random House, 2001).

6. See Dan Ariely, *Predictably Irrational* (New York: Harper Collins, 2008). Ariely discusses numerous examples like the above, including the Amazon.com shipping policy.

7. Antonio Damasio, *Descartes' Error* (New York: Harper Collins, 1995) p. xv.

8. Ibid., pp. 44–45.

9. Ibid., p. xvii.

10. For a fascinating and influential discussion of this theme, see Jonathan Bennett, "The Conscience of Huckleberry Finn," *Philosophy* 49 (1974): 123–134.

11. David Hume, *A Treatise of Human Nature*, ed. L. A. Selby-Bigge, rev. P. H. Nidditch (Oxford: Oxford University Press, 1978), p. 415.

12. Ibid, p. 416.

13. The literature on the so-called basic emotions is huge; for a tip of the iceberg see P. Ekman, "The Argument and Evidence About Universals in Facial Expressions of Emotion," in H. Wagner and A. Manstead, eds., *Handbook of Social Psychophysiology: The Biological Psychology of the Emotions and Social Processes* (New York: John Wiley and Sons, 1989), pp. 143–164. Ekman expanded his list of basic emotions in his "Basic emotions," *The Handbook of Cognition and Emotion*, ed. T. Dalgleish and T. Power (New York: John Wiley and Sons, 1999), pp. 45–60.

14. As Catherine Elgin puts it, emotions can be justified and unjustified; see her *Considered Judgment* (Princeton: Princeton University Press, 1996), p. 149.

15. Indeed, if emotions can serve as "markers" that indicate to us salient aspects of a particular situation, they are in some sense akin to perceptions. And thus, like perceptions, they can be criticized when they don't reflect how the situation actually is. If the situation is not one that calls for anger, or gaiety or grief, then having these feelings doesn't make sense in something like the way that seeing a pink elephant in the room when there isn't one doesn't make sense. For theories that take emotions to be closely linked or identical to perceptions, see R. de Sousa, *The Rationality of Emotion* (Cambridge, Mass.: MIT Press, 1990); D. Sosa, "Skepticism about Intuition" *Philosophy* (2006) 88: 633–648. J. J. Prinz, *Gut Reactions: A Perceptual Theory of Emotion* (Oxford: Oxford University Press, 2004).

16. Simon Blackburn, perhaps the most prominent defender of the Humean picture now writing, makes this point in his *Ruling Passions* (Oxford: Oxford University Press, 1998), p. 265. The sophisticated Humean can say: were your motivational profile more coherent, you wouldn't be motivated to do so and so.

17. For an elaboration of this theory, see M. Lynch, "Trusting Intuition," in P. Greenough and M. Lynch, eds., *Realism and Truth* (Oxford: Oxford University Press, 2006).

18. To intuit something isn't just to believe it. We can believe what we don't find intuitive and can intuit what we don't believe. Example: I find it very intuitive that, for anything whatsoever, there is a set that contains that thing as a member; but I know that this idea leads to a contradiction. So I don't believe it. (Proof for homework: is there a set of all sets that are not members of themselves?)

19. Haidt, "The Emotional Dog and Its Rational Tail," p. 818.

20. T. Hoving, *False Impressions: The Hunt for Big Time Art Fakes* (New York: Touchstone Press, 2006), p. 19.

21. M. Polanyi, *Personal Knowledge: Toward a Post-Critical Philosophy* (Chicago: University of Chicago Press, 1974).

22. See Haidt, "The Emotional Dog and Its Rational Tail," p. 820.

23. Ibid., p. 819.

24. Drew Westen, *The Political Brain: The Role of Emotion in Deciding the Fate of the Nation* (New York: Public Affairs, 2007), p. xv.

25. Ibid., pp. 111–112.

26. Ibid., p. 112.

27. W. V. O. Quine, "Two Dogmas of Empiricism," in his *From a Logical Point of View* (Cambridge, Mass.: Harvard University Press, 1953), pp. 2–3.

28. Ibid.

29. Haidt, "The Emotional Dog and Its Rational Tail," pp. 814–834.

30. Lincoln Quillian, "Group Threat and Regional Change in Attitudes Toward African-Americans," *American Journal of Sociology* 102 (1996), p. 826.

31. Ibid., p. 827.

## 3  "Nothing but Dreams and Smoke"

1. Richard Popkin, *The History of Skepticism from Savonarola to Bayle* (Oxford: Oxford University Press, 2003), p. 18.

2. See Popkin, *History of Skepticism*; and Terence Penelhum, *God and Skepticism: A Study in Skepticism and Fideism* (Dordrecht: D. Reidel, 1983).

3. Michel de Montaigne, *Apology for Raymond Sebond*, trans. R. Ariew and M. Greene (Indianapolis: Hackett, 2003), p. 50.

4. Ibid., p. 102.

5. The exact date of the event is open to debate. Here, I follow Richard Popkin who places it in 1628; see his *History of Skepticism*, p. 147. Some, including Desmond Clarke, indicate it may have happened in the autumn of the previous year; see Clarke, *Descartes: A Biography* (Cambridge: Cambridge University Press, 2006), p. 423.

6. In Descartes, *Discourse on Method*; see Popkin, *History of Skepticism*, p. 145.

7. René Descartes, *Meditations on First Philosophy*, trans. J. Cottingham (Cambridge: Cambridge University Press, 1986), p. 12.

8. Descartes took himself to have a reply to the charge of circularity, although the exact nature of that reply remains controversial. His response can be found in "The Fourth Replies" in *The Philosophical Writings of Descartes*, vol. 2, ed. J. Cottingham, R. Stoothoff, D. Murdoch, and A. Kenny (Cambridge: Cambridge University Press, 1991). The literature on the alleged circle is vast. See Michael Della Rocca, "Descartes, the Cartesian Circle, and Epistemology Without God," *Philosophy and Phenomenological Research* 70 (2005), pp. 1–33; Louis E. Loeb, "The Cartesian Circle," in *The Cambridge Companion to Descartes*, ed. John Cottingham (Cambridge: Cambridge University Press, 1992); Ernest Sosa, "How to Resolve the Pyrrhonian Problematic: A Lesson from Descartes," *Philosophical Studies* 85 (1997), pp. 229–249.

9. David Hume, *Enquiry Concerning Human Understanding*, ed. T. Beauchamp (Oxford: Oxford University Press, 1999), p. 199 (§ 12, 1).

10. This sometimes seems to have been missed by Montaigne, whose catchphrase—which he had printed on coins bearing his image, no less—was "What do I know?" It is not, I think, missed by Steven Hales, whose seminal *Relativism and the Foundations of Philosophy* (Cambridge,

Mass.: MIT Press, 2006) presents a similar argument from what I call below "epistemic incommensurability" to a form of epistemic relativism.

11. See Ernest Sosa's *Apt Belief and Reflective Knowledge*, 2 vols. (Oxford: Oxford University Press, 2007, 2009); see particularly, chapters 7 and 8 in vol. 2, *Reflective Knowledge*. Ideas similar to Sosa's have been kicked around by many philosophers from different traditions. Michael Polanyi talked about "tacit knowledge," and Sosa himself has argued that the basic idea can be traced throughout modern philosophy. In more recent times, the possibility of animal knowledge is most closely associated with externalist views in epistemology.

12. See, e.g., the Second Set of Replies in *The Philosophical Writings of Descartes,* ed. J. Cottingham, R. Stoothoff, and D. Murdoch (New York: Cambridge University Press, 1985), vol. II, p. 101.

13. See Sosa, *Apt Belief and Reflective Knowledge*, vol. 1, pp. 130–131.

14. Philosophers often call the type of circularity in question here "epistemic circularity." This is meant to distinguish it from "premise circularity," in which the argument is circular because the conclusion appears (if in veiled form) in the premises. An argument is epistemically circular, in contrast, if we must be committed to the truth of the conclusion in order to be justified in accepting the premises. The *locus classicus* for discussion of this issue is W. P. Alston's *The Reliability of Sense Perception* (Ithaca: Cornell University Press, 1993).

15. As Alston notes (ibid., p. 19), it does no good to protest that one can justify vision's reliability by appeal to, e.g., hearing and touch—for how do we justify their reliability, in turn, without at some point relying on vision?

16. Can't I just use a simple track-record argument for the reliability of deduction? Perhaps. But note that, even putting aside the question of the modal strength of deduction's reliability, there is the following problem. Track-record arguments presuppose an obvious deductive inference from the following principle: If T is a track-record argument, and T shows that M is reliable, then M is reliable. Without the relevant

inference in play as a presupposition, track-record arguments are irrelevant to the reliability of deductive inference. With it in play, they are epistemically circular.

17. Including perhaps some of those involved in the Texas State School Board; see Russell Shorto, "How Christian Were the Founders?" *New York Times Magazine* (February 11, 2010), p. 35.

18. Smith could of course try to give some independent argument, in addition to the one I've given above, in defense of his principle—one that does not rely on what the Bible says. He might appeal to the teaching of various prophets, or other sacred texts. Jones will question the reliability of these sources. So Smith might appeal to still more basic, noninferential methods of belief formation, such as divine revelation or a mystical perception of God's actions and will. But here again the question can (and presumably will) be raised about the reliability of such methods. As Hales (*Relativism and the Foundations of Philosophy*, pp. 53–54) has argued, it is difficult to see how Smith will be able to demonstrate these methods' reliability without employing a circular argument, for it is difficult to see how one could defend one's claims to reliably speak for or perceive God without appealing either to the Bible, or to mystic perception again.

19. Contrast Thomas Nagel, in *The Last Word* (Oxford: Oxford University Press, 1996), p. 5: "To reason is to think systematically in ways anyone looking over my shoulder ought to be able to recognize as correct." Unlike the present account, Nagel holds this as a condition on reasoning simpliciter, not just the giving of reasons.

20. The Kuhnian term was suggested to me by Duncan Pritchard some years ago. For Pritchard's own take on the problem, see his "Epistemic Relativism, Epistemic Incommensurability, and Wittgensteinian Epistemology," in *A Companion to Relativism*, ed. S. Hales (Oxford: Wiley-Blackwell, 2011), pp. 266–285. See also Boghossian, *Fear of Knowledge* (Oxford: Oxford University Press, 2004), pp. 118–121.

21. This is the sort of response one might expect from those who ascribe to what is called "externalism" in epistemology. But as I argue in the text, I have no quarrel with externalists about knowledge—at least for

the purposes of this book. The issue here isn't knowledge; it is the role of reason. For discussion of externalism and skepticism within the context of epistemic circularity, see Richard Fumerton, *Metaepistemology and Skepticism* (Boston: Rowman & Littlefield, 1996), pp. 159–181; Barry Stroud, "Scepticism, 'Externalism,' and the Goal of Epistemology," *Aristotelian Society Supplementary Volume* 68 (1994), pp. 291–307; Duncan Pritchard, *Epistemic Luck* (Oxford: Clarendon Press, 2007), pp. 208–213; B. Reed, "Epistemic Circularity Squared? Skepticism about Common Sense," *Philosophy and Phenomenological Research* 73 (2006): 186–197; Ernest Sosa, "How to Resolve the Pyrrhonian Problematic: A Lesson from Descartes," *Philosophical Studies* 85 (1997): 229–249; and Sosa's "Reflective Knowledge in the Best of Circles," *Journal of Philosophy* 94 (1997): 410–430.

22. It would be like telling someone faced with a moral dilemma—where, e.g., the demands of utility clash with respect for persons—not to worry because, "if you act on the correct moral principles, you'll do the right thing." Thanks a lot.

23. The issue here is also not that generally discussed under the heading of "the epistemology of peer disagreement." That is a debate about what conclusions we should draw when confronted with someone we regard as epistemic and intellectual peers but with whom we disagree about some matter about which we are equally informed. Where you and I disagree over the truth of some fundamental epistemic principle, however, we will not be able to regard each other as epistemic peers, even if we regard each other as intellectual ones. For your fundamental epistemic principles concern basic methods of belief. And which basic methods of belief you think are reliable will determine what you count as evidence. Thus you won't regard someone with whom you disagree about a fundamental epistemic principle as having the same evidence as you, simply because they will be, from your point of view, ignoring methods that would give them such evidence. Consider, by way of example, our creationist. He will not regard me as an epistemic peer, for I don't have the same evidence as him precisely because I don't consult the Bible (or lack divine inspiration or some such). For discussion of the epistemology of peer disagreement, see Thomas Kelly, "The Epistemic

Significance of Disagreement," in T. S. Gendler and J. Hawthorne, eds., *Oxford Studies in Epistemology*, vol. 1 (Oxford: Oxford University Press, 2005), pp. 167–196; Richard Feldman, "Reasonable Religious Disagreements," in Louise Antony, ed., *Philosophers without Gods: Meditations on Atheism and the Secular Life* (Oxford: Oxford University Press, 2007), pp. 194–214; and David Christensen, "Epistemology of Disagreement: The Good News," *Philosophical Review* 116, no. 2 (2007): 187–217.

## 4   Reasons End: Tradition and Common Sense

1. Thomas Kuhn, *The Structure of Scientific Revolutions* (Chicago: University of Chicago Press, 1962), p. 109.

2. Alasdair MacIntyre, *Whose Justice? Which Rationality?* (Notre Dame: University of Notre Dame Press, 1988), p. 367. This passage seems at odds with some of MacIntyre's previous comments on tradition and fideism. For discussion, see Mark Mitchell, "Michael Polanyi, Alasdair MacIntyre, and the Role of Tradition," *Humanitas* 19 (2006): 97–125.

3. Michael Oakeshott, "Reason and the Conduct of Political Life," in his *Rationalism in Politics and Other Essays* (Indianapolis: Liberty Fund, 1991), p. 56.

4. Oakeshott, *Rationalism in Politics*, p. 37.

5. Kuhn, *Structure*, p. 151.

6. Ibid., p. 150.

7. Ibid., p. 109.

8. Richard Rorty, "Universality and Truth," in *Rorty and His Critics*, ed. R. B. Brandom (Oxford: Blackwell, 2000), p. 20.

9. Some forms of relativism may avoid this charge; see Steven Hales's view in his *Relativism and the Foundations of Philosophy* (Cambridge, Mass.: MIT Press, 2005). Of course, relativisms that do avoid it may not be worth calling "relativist"; but what is in a word?

10. Ludwig Wittgenstein, *On Certainty*, ed. and trans. G. E. M. Anscombe and G. H. von Wright (Oxford: Blackwell, 1969), §110. For

commentary on these and related passages, see Michael Williams, *Unnatural Doubts: Epistemological Realism and the Basis of Scepticism* (Oxford: Blackwell, 1991); and Duncan Pritchard, "Wittgenstein on Scepticism," in *The Oxford Handbook of Wittgenstein*, ed. O. Kuusela and M. McGinn (Oxford: Oxford University Press, 2011).

11. Wittgenstein, *On Certainty*, §205.

12. Ibid., §§341–343.

13. Ibid., §264.

14. Wittgenstein, *On Certainty*, §§611–612. See also Duncan Pritchard, "Epistemic Relativism, Epistemic Incommensurability, and Wittgensteinian Epistemology," in *The Blackwell Companion to Relativism*, ed. S. Hales (Cambridge: Blackwell, 2011), pp. 266–285.

15. We need something in common that we can settle on. Traditionalists of course may insist that we do have something in common: a common tradition. We live in a Christian nation, they might say: "One nation under God" (a slogan put on U.S. currency in the 1950s). But not everyone would agree. I don't, for example.

16. This appears to be MacIntyre's position; see *Whose Justice? Which Rationality?*, pp. 351–352.

17. David Hume, *An Enquiry Concerning Human Understanding*, ed. T. Beauchamp (Oxford: Oxford University Press, 1999), pp. 121 (§5, 4–5).

18. Ibid., pp. 123–124 (§5, 8).

19. Thomas Reid, *Inquiry into the Human Mind*, ed. D. R. Brookes (Edinburgh: Edinburgh University Press, 1997), p. 33. An excellent discussion of Reid's commonsense epistemology can be found in N. Wolterstorff's *Thomas Reid and the Story of Epistemology* (Cambridge: Cambridge University Press, 2001), especially pp. 215–216.

20. William Alston suggests a strategy similar to the one I've credited to Reid: "there is no alternative (practically rational or otherwise) to using in an investigation what we accept . . . as reliable belief-forming practices and probably true beliefs." Alston's point is that we always

have to take some principles or others for granted. It is not entirely clear
whether Alston thinks that this fact itself carries epistemic or practical
weight. In any event, as I argue in the text, the "no alternative" point,
although an important step in the right direction, doesn't always suffice
to explain how we can give reasons to each other for our most basic
principles when challenged. Alston, *Beyond "Justification"* (Ithaca, N.Y.:
Cornell University Press, 2005), p. 221. See also Hales, *Relativism and the
Foundations of Philosophy*, p 85; Boghossion, *Fear of Knowledge*.

21. John M. Frame, "Presuppositional Apologetics," in *Five Views on
Apologetics*, ed. S. N. Gundry and S. B. Cowan (Grand Rapids, Mich.:
Zondervan, 2000), p. 217.

22. Romans 1.19–20.

23. Vincent Cheung, "Professional Morons," 2005. You can still access
Cheung's writings on his webpage: http://www.vincentcheung.com.

24. This point would also weigh against an attempt to use Crispin
Wright's influential work on skepticism about knowledge to answer the
quite different skeptic about reason with whom we are concerned in
this essay. Wright's basic thought is that we are entitled to certain principles. To be entitled in Wright's sense is, roughly, to have epistemic
warrant for a proposition without having any epistemic reasons to
believe it. One is entitled to a proposition in this sense when (a) that
proposition is presupposed by one's cognitive projects; (b) one has no
reason to think it is not true; and (c) any attempt to justify it would rest
on propositions whose epistemic standing is no better off. Perhaps we
are entitled in this sense to our fundamental principles. And perhaps,
as Wright suggests, entitlement is epistemic and not pragmatic in character—it provides what we are calling justification for a belief. If so, then
certain forms of skepticism may be false. So, this proposal has significant
merits; but it does not allow us to provide an epistemically rational reso-
lution of deep epistemic disagreements. Suppose, for example, that
Smith (the young-earth creationist from chapter 3) tells you that he is
entitled to his fundamental epistemic principles. This may well be so.
We can imagine that treating a holy book as the most reliable guide to
the past *is* presupposed by one of his basic cognitive projects—like

understanding the will of God. And he sees no reason to think it is unreliable. I doubt you will be moved unless you accept Smith's cognitive project. You may even feel that, from your standpoint, you can offer a reason to believe that Smith's methods are unreliable, and therefore that his fundamental epistemic principles are false. But of course, whether this is so is the very issue you and Smith are disagreeing about. If your epistemic disagreement is truly deep, you won't recognize each other's epistemic reasons in the domain of belief in question precisely because those reasons themselves are produced by sources whose reliability is in question. In short, "I'm entitled to P" cannot be used to *give* a reason for P in a case of deep epistemic disagreement, *even if* the person who is entitled is warranted in holding P. See Crispin Wright, "Warrant for Nothing (and Foundations for Free)?" in *Proceedings of the Aristotelian Society Supplementary Volume* 78, no. 1 (2004): 167–212.

## 5 The "Sacred Tradition of Humanity"

1. The School of Mathematics and Statistics at the University of St. Andrews, Scotland, where Clifford once taught, has a useful short article on Clifford's mathematical life: "William Kingdon Clifford" by J. J. O'Connor and E. F. Robertson; see http://www-history.mcs.st-and.ac.uk/history/Biographies/Clifford.html.

2. W. K. Clifford, initially published in the *Contemporary Review*; pages here refer to *The Ethics of Belief and Other Essays*, intro. T. Madigan (Amherst, N.Y.: Prometheus Books, 1999).

3. David Berlinski, *The Devil's Delusion: Atheism and Its Scientific Pretensions* (New York: Crown Forum, 2008), p. 47.

4. Clifford, *The Ethics of Belief*, p. 76.

5. Ibid., p. 91.

6. Try this one at home: try believing, *right now*, that you have a blue flower growing out of your head. Believe it? Hardly. You may say the words "I've got a blue flower growing out of my head," and you may get as far as imagining that you do. But you can't just will yourself to

believe it any more than I can will myself to believe I am better looking than George Clooney, or smarter than Einstein. Whether you feel that something is true is simply not up to you. Consequently, it doesn't really make sense to say that your beliefs are morally wrong any more than it makes sense to say that your feeling sad or happy is morally wrong.

7. What I'm calling "commitment" here is drawn from L. Jonathan Cohen's notion of "acceptance"; see his *An Essay on Belief and Acceptance* (Oxford: Oxford University Press, 1992), p. 4.

8. The difference between belief and commitment is often overlooked. This is partly due to the fact that the word "belief" does double duty in ordinary conversation. Most of the time, we take it to mean our disposition to feel that some proposition or other is true. In this sense, beliefs are like any other feelings: they are not under the control of the will. But sometimes we use "belief" to indicate an active state of mind, as when we talk of "refusing to believe" or "choosing to believe." Here we are thinking of a state of mind that we *do* have control over, and while this state of mind can be confused with belief, the two aren't the same. This act is better called a "commitment."

9. For similar remarks about rational trust, see Crispin Wright, "Warrant for Nothing (and Foundations for Free)?" in *Aristotelian Society Supplementary Volume* 78, no. 1 (2004): 167–212.

10. W. P. Alston argued for a similar strategy. The most practically rational methods are those "most firmly rooted in our lives" (*The Reliability of Sense Perception* [Ithaca: Cornell University Press, 1993], p. 125). Thus, where we find that principles conflict, "we should give preference to the more firmly established practice," where this means, among other things, favoring a practice that is more "widely accepted" and "more important," that has "a more innate basis" and is "more difficult to abstain from" (ibid., p. 136). As we'll see, Alston's last two points bear further looking into; I will suggest something similar. However, his first several criteria are, to my mind, unhelpful. It is difficult to see how, without begging questions, we could say which of two competing fundamental epistemic principles is more "widely accepted" or "more

important." Moreover, being "widely accepted" doesn't seem to be a *good* practical reason for favoring one practice over another. Indeed, depending on who is doing the accepting, it can be a bad reason. Moreover, as I suggested in chapter 4, it is not clear how an appeal to social entrenchment is going to deliver public reasons that can, at least hypothetically, help us adjudicate disputes over epistemic principles.

11. See Brian Deer, "MMR Doctor Andrew Wakefield Fixed Data on Autism," *Sunday Times* (February 8, 2009); G. A. Poland and R. M. Jacobson, "The Age-Old Struggle against the Antivaccinationists," *New England Journal of Medicine* 364, no. 2 (Jan. 2011): 97–99.

12. See Helen E. Longino, *Science as Social Knowledge: Values and Objectivity in Scientific Inquiry* (Princeton: Princeton University Press, 1990), p. 69.

13. See Nicholas Wade, "Harvard Finds Scientist Guilty of Misconduct," *New York Times* (Aug. 20, 2010), p. A1, and "Scientist Under Inquiry Resigns from Harvard" (July 20, 2011), p. A17.

14. There are, of course, deep issues here about the nature of scientific realism. For an excellent discussion in line with the present approach, see Philip Kitcher's *Science, Truth, and Democracy* (Oxford: Oxford University Press, 2001), chap. 2.

15. See Longino, *Science as Social Knowledge*, pp. 62–63.

16. Of course, I am *not* claiming that the openness and objectivity of an epistemic principle means it is true. Moreover, the fact that a principle is open to some degree and can be objectively assessed isn't a neutral *epistemic* reason in its favor. If you and I disagree over a truly fundamental epistemic principle, I probably won't be able to convince you it is true by appealing to the fact that it is open to being publicly assessed. I might be able to convince you, however, that such principles are more practically rational.

17. PAST is hardly the only example of a fundamental comparative principle. Another example is:

INTROSPECTION:   The most reliable method for learning about our conscious mental states is by introspecting those states.

This is a controversial position in the philosophy of psychology. For discussion (and criticism of the principle), see Hilary Kornblith, *Knowledge and Its Place in Nature* (Oxford: Clarendon Press, 2002), chap. 4.

18. John Rawls, *A Theory of Justice* (Cambridge, Mass.: Harvard University Press, 1971), p. 11.

19. This modification of Rawls was initially inspired by a conversation with the philosopher Eberhard Herrmann while we walked near his home in Sweden.

20. Complicating decisions with regard to the base set, and subsequent decisions (see below) about how to weight principles included in that set, will be issues of consistency and coherence between its members, and how to understand those notions. We can, if we like, imagine the players having to readjust the relevant principles in light of worries about consistency.

21. "Seeming effectiveness" because, from the standpoint of playing the game, we can't judge whether the methods *are* effective.

22. Alston raises a parallel worry when he says: "But the fact remains that where making a reasoned choice as to what modes of belief formation to employ, there is no question of doing so without already having [fundamental epistemic principles] at our disposal without having chosen them on the basis of reasons" (*Beyond "Justification"* [Ithaca: Cornell University Press, 2005], pp. 219–220). So, he adds, it would be "arbitrary" to temporarily privilege some epistemic principles over others, since in doing so we'll already be appealing to some principles. In fact, this is not a worry for the method game as I've presented it. As I make clear in the text, I am perfectly willing to allow for the obvious fact that all players of the game will come to the table with a set of epistemic commitments.

23. William P. Alston, *The Reliability of Sense Perception* (Ithaca: Cornell University Press, 1993), p. 132.

24. One might object by claiming that to know that P requires that it be epistemically rational to believe that P, and that the reasons the method game gives us for our epistemic principles are not epistemic.

No doubt. But the present question is not the way in which our epistemic commitments are rational, but whether the beliefs produced by the methods of belief those commitments are about are rational. The present argument is this: If it is rational simpliciter to trust a given method of belief-formation, then the beliefs this method produces are rational; and beliefs which are produced by trustworthy methods are, prima facie, *epistemically* rational.

25. See Michael Fuerstein, "The Scientific Public: Inquiry in Democratic Society," Ph.D. dissertation, Columbia University, 2009.

## 6 Truth and the Pathos of Distance

1. Richard Rorty, "Response to Williams," in *Rorty and His Critics*, ed. R. B. Brandom (Cambridge: Blackwell, 2000), p. 217.

2. Richard Rorty, "Response to Ramberg," in *Rorty and His Critics*, p. 375.

3. Richard Rorty, "Universality and Truth," in *Rorty and His Critics*, p. 7.

4. Ibid., p. 2.

5. Ibid., p. 4.

6. Simon Blackburn, *Spreading the Word* (Oxford: Oxford University Press, 1984); for a different view, see G. Vision, *Veritas* (Cambridge, Mass.: MIT Press, 2004).

7. Typically, the thought is that we employ a mental representational analog of a Tarskian recursive truth definition, and define the truth of a mental content in terms of something analogous to satisfaction, predicate application and denotation. See H. Field, "Tarski's Theory of Truth," *Journal of Philosophy* 69 (1972): 347–375; and M. Devitt, *Realism and Truth* (Princeton: Princeton University Press, 1984).

8. Obviously, this is only the barest hint of a theory. Among other things, causal isomorphism alone is insufficient for accurate representation. One reason for this is that a map of the London Underground can be structurally isomorphic with tons of things: configurations of blades of grass, canyons on Mars, the tunnels in an anthill. So what makes my

map a map of the London Underground isn't just shared structural relationships. What needs to be added to get over these problems is of course the subject of a thriving industry. See, e.g., M. Devitt, *Designation* (New York: Columbia University Press, 1981), and *Realism and Truth*, 2nd ed. (Princeton: Princeton University Press, 1997). See also F. Dretske, *Knowledge and the Flow of Information* (Cambridge, Mass.: MIT Press, 1981); R. Millikan, *Language, Thought and Other Biological Categories* (Cambridge, Mass.: MIT Press, 1984); and J. Fodor, *Psychosemantics* (Cambridge, Mass.: MIT Press, 1987).

9. For my elaboration and defense of this point with regard to claims of value, see "The Values of Truth and the Truth of Values," in *Epistemic Value*, ed. A. Haddock, A. Millar, and D. Pritchard (Oxford: Oxford University Press, 2010).

10. Deflationists will of course allow that this is not what is going on in cases of generalizations like "Everything Socrates said was true." But this, says the deflationist, helps make their point: the only function of "true" is to help us make such generalizations and therefore spare us the tiresome (and perhaps impossible) task of repeating everything old Socrates might have said. See Paul Horwich, *Truth*, 2nd edition (Oxford: Oxford University Press, 1998).

11. Richard Rorty, *Consequences of Pragmatism* (Minneapolis: University of Minnesota Press, 1982), p. xiii.

12. See my "Minimalism and the Value of Truth," *Philosophical Quarterly* 54 (2004): 497–517; for an important criticism of deflationism, see Anil Gupta, "A Critique of Deflationism," *Philosophical Topics* 21 (1993): 53–81.

13. The idea that there can be more than one property that plays the truth-role requires, of course, significant technical development; see my *Truth as One and Many* (Oxford: Oxford University Press, 2009). I first presented this view in my essay, "A Functionalist Theory of Truth," in *The Nature of Truth*, ed. M. P. Lynch (Cambridge, Mass.: MIT Press, 2001); see also my "Truth and Multiple Realizability," *Australasian Journal of Philosophy* 82 (2004): 384–408.

14. The idea of supercoherence stems from Crispin Wright's notion of "superassertibility" as defined in his *Truth and Objectivity* (Cambridge, Mass.: Harvard University Press, 1992), and from the earlier ideas of C. S. Peirce. For a discussion of Peirce, see Cheryl Misak, *Truth and the End of Inquiry* (Oxford: Oxford University Press, 2004).

15. A belief-system is *coherent* to the degree it "hangs together," as Sellars says—that is, to the degree that its component beliefs collectively and individually support each other deductively and inductively. A "stage of inquiry," as the phrase suggests, is a state of warranted information or evidence. Stages are understood as being extensible (additional information might always come in) and inclusive (the additional information is just that—additional; all successive stages of inquiry include the information warranted at prior stages). The reader will note that our condition leaves room for the plausible thought that stages of inquiry are potentially incomplete: that is, to hold that relative to a given stage of inquiry, neither a belief nor its negation will be supercoherent. Coupled with the idea that supercoherence plays the truth-role, this entails a rejection of the law of excluded middle or the thought that P or not P, together with associated inferences, such as double-negation elimination. This is a much-discussed topic; two recent treatments include Wright, *Truth and Objectivity*, pp. 37–38; JC Beall and Greg Restall, *Logical Pluralism* (Oxford: Oxford University Press, 2006).

16. Richard Rorty, "True to Life: Why Truth Matters," *Philosophy and Phenomenological Research* 71 (2005), pp. 231–239.

17. A more detailed version of this point can be found in my *Truth as One and Many* (Oxford: Oxford University Press, 2009), pp. 41–42.

18. This point was anticipated by Russell: "the objection to the coherence theory lies in this, that it presupposes a more usual meaning of truth and falsehood in constructing its coherent whole, and that more usual meaning, though indispensable to the theory, cannot be explained in terms of the theory." Bertrand Russell, "The Monistic Theory of Truth," reprinted in his *Philosophical Essays* (London: George Allen & Unwin, 1966), p. 136.

19. Thus, in a very real sense, we can't avoid doing ontological heavy lifting for some of the propositions that philosophers have found troubling, because we are going to have to say what makes it the case that it is true that some beliefs are coherent and some not. But that is a task for another time.

## Conclusion

1. This is the theme in George Lakoff's *Whose Freedom? The Battle over America's Most Important Idea* (New York: Farrar, Straus & Giroux, 2006); see, e.g., p. 15.

2. See, e.g., Michael Savage's charmingly named *Liberalism Is a Mental Disorder: Savage Solutions* (Nashville: Thomas Nelson, 2005).

# Index